STARTUP
BOARDS

STARTUP
BOARDS

A Field Guide to Building and Leading
an Effective Board of Directors

Second Edition

Brad Feld
Matt Blumberg
Mahendra Ramsinghani

WILEY

Published by John Wiley & Sons, Inc., Hoboken, New Jersey.

Published simultaneously in Canada.

For general information on our other products and services or for technical support, please contact our Customer Care Department within the United States at (800) 762-2974, outside the United States at (317) 572-3993 or fax (317) 572-4002.

Wiley also publishes its books in a variety of electronic formats. Some content that appears in print may not be available in electronic formats. For more information about Wiley products, visit our web site at www.wiley.com.

Library of Congress Cataloging-in-Publication Data

Names: Feld, Brad, author. | Blumberg, Matt, author. | Ramsinghani,
    Mahendra, author.
Title: Startup boards : a field guide to building and leading an effective
    board of directors / Brad Feld, Matt Blumberg, Mahendra Ramsinghani.
Description: Second edition. | Hoboken, New Jersey : Wiley, 2022. |
    Includes bibliographical references and index.
Identifiers: LCCN 2022010446 (print) | LCCN 2022010447 (ebook) | ISBN
    9781119859284 (cloth) | ISBN 9781119859307 (adobe pdf) | ISBN
    9781119859291 (epub)
Subjects: LCSH: New business enterprises—Management. | Boards of
    directors. | Entrepreneurship.
Classification: LCC HD62.5 .F44 2022 (print) | LCC HD62.5 (ebook) | DDC
    658.1/1—dc23/eng/20220304
LC record available at https://lccn.loc.gov/2022010446
LC ebook record available at https://lccn.loc.gov/2022010447

Cover Design: Wiley
Cover Image: © Ani_Ka/Getty Images

SKY10034030_042122

Contents

Foreword   xiii

Preface   xvii

SECTION 1: Board Fundamentals   1

Chapter 1: Introduction   3
What's New in the Second Edition   4
Who This Book Is For   6
Magic Words, Phrases, Abbreviations, and Style   7
Note   9

Chapter 2: The Board's Purpose   11
Accountability   12
General Responsibilities   12

Chapter 3: Legal Characteristics   15
A Board Member's Legal Duties   16
Addressing Conflicting Duties   18
Benefit Corporations and the B Corp Movement   20
Should You Get D&O Insurance?   21
Note   23

Chapter 4: Board Member Roles   25
Chair or Lead Director   25
Executive Chair   28

Should You Be Chair of Your Board?   29

Independent Board Members   30

Board Observers   30

Outside Counsel   32

Note   34

Chapter 5: Board Functions   **35**

The Role of Board Committees   35

Informal Responsibilities of a Board   36

Control Priorities   37

Being Rich and Queen (or King)   39

Shareholder Rights   40

Economic and Performance Priorities   41

Emotional Priorities: Trust, Judgment, and Transparency 42

Notes   43

SECTION 2: Creating Your Board   **45**

Chapter 6: Size and Composition   **47**

Management   48

Investors   49

Independents   50

Matt's Rule of 1s   51

Notes   52

Chapter 7: VCs and Boards   **53**

Notes   56

Chapter 8: Board Evolution   **57**

Startup Stages   57

Limiting the Number of Investor Board Members   59

Managing Independent Seats   60

Chapter 9: What to Look for in a Director   **63**

General Skills   63

Fit with Your Existing Board   64

What Does Your Company Need?   65

Experiences   66

Attributes   69

Governance Philosophy   69

Chapter 10: Recruiting and Interviewing Board Members   **71**

Sourcing   71

The Interview Process   73

Interviewing VCs Before They Join Your Board   76

Chapter 11: Compensation   **77**

VCs and Management   77

Independent Directors   78

Notes   80

Chapter 12: Board Diversity   **81**

Unconscious Bias   81

The First Step: Appoint Independent Directors Early   83

The Second Step: Open Your Search to Board-Ready
First-Timers   83

Notes   86

Chapter 13: Onboarding Your Directors   87

Using Employee Onboarding as a Guide   87

Onboarding New Directors   88

Interacting with Your Team   89

Chapter 14: Removing a Board Member   91

Removing a Founder Director   92

Removing an Investor Director   92

Removing an Independent Director   93

Getting Rid of the Entire Board   94

Notes   95

Chapter 15: Is an Advisory Board Useful?   97

Board of Directors vs. Advisory Board   98

Attributes of a Useful Advisory Board Member   99

Selecting Advisory Board Members   100

Building an Advisory Board   100

Challenges of Advisory Boards   101

Notes   102

SECTION 3: Preparing for and Running the Board Meeting   103

Chapter 16: Preparing for the Board Meeting   105

The Value of Preparation   106

The Meeting Agenda   107

Focus on Critical Items   108

The Board Book   109

Creating an Annual Calendar   113

Notes   114

Chapter 17: Meeting Dynamics   **115**

Seating   115

The Meeting Length   116

Including Your Team in the Board Meeting   117

Slides or No Slides?   118

Discussion or Decision Item?   118

The Executive Session and the Closed Session   119

A Board Call Instead of a Meeting   120

Remote Attendees and Hybrid Meetings   121

The Post-Meeting Survey   123

Post Meeting   124

Notes   125

Chapter 18: Motions and Votes   **127**

Robert's Rules of Order   127

Have Your Lawyer at the Meeting   128

The Mechanics of Voting   128

What If You Don't Agree?   129

Dealing with Formal Items   130

Minutes   131

Unanimous Written Consent   131

Notes   132

SECTION 4: Between Meetings: Ongoing Work   **133**

Chapter 19: Managing Ongoing Communication   **135**

What the Board Expects from a CEO   135

Communicate Both Good and Bad News   136

Note   138

Chapter 20: Committees   **139**

Committee Meeting Formalities   139

Compensation   140

Audit   141

Nominating   142

CEO Expenses   142

Chapter 21: Mentors and Learning by Doing   **145**

Mentorship and Vulnerability   145

Learning by Doing   147

Chapter 22: CEO Transitions   **149**

Situations That Lead to a CEO Change   149

Scale Up with Growth   151

Why Boards Fire CEOs   152

Planning for Healthy Transitions   154

Notes   155

SECTION 5: Transactions   **157**

Chapter 23: Financings   **159**

New Investor-Led Round   159

Insider-Led Round   160

The Down Round and a Rights Offering   161

How Involved Should VCs Be in Financings?   161

Convertible Notes   162

Venture Debt   162

Notes   163

Chapter 24: Stock Option Grants and 409A Valuations   **165**

Chapter 25: Selling a Company   **169**

Confidentiality   169

Fiduciary Responsibility   170

Your Outside Counsel's Role   171

Acquihire   172

Carve-Outs and 280G   173

Shareholder Representative   173

Note   174

Chapter 26: Buying a Company   **175**

Negotiating and Structuring the Deal   175

Financing an Acquisition   176

Board Approvals   177

Managing Transaction and Post-Deal Integration   178

Chapter 27: Going Public   **179**

Process   179

Committees   180

Confidentiality   180

Insider Status   181

VCs on Public Company Boards   181

SPACs   182

Chapter 28: Going Out of Business   **185**

The Zone of Insolvency   185

Responsibility to Creditors   186

Responsibility to Shareholders   187

Liability   188

Chapter 11   188

Chapter 7   189

Assignment for the Benefit of Creditors   189

**SECTION 6: For Independent Directors and Aspiring
Board Members**   **191**

Chapter 29: Preparing for Your First Board Role   **193**

Note   196

Chapter 30: Interviewing for a Board Role   **197**

The Interview   197

Diligence Items to Explore   198

Chapter 31: Your First Board Meeting   **201**

Chapter 32: Communicating Effectively   **205**

Note   208

Chapter 33: How to Be a Great Board Member   **209**

Chapter 34: Conclusion   **213**

Acknowledgments   215

Bibliography   217

Index   221

Foreword

I was honored when Brad, Matt, and Mahendra asked me to write the Foreword for the second edition of *Startup Boards*. As the CEO of Him for Her, I've worked closely with Brad and Matt. They are iconic leaders who have done much to promote entrepreneurship. I also read the first edition of *Startup Boards* and found it to be a helpful outlay for venture-backed boards, so I responded with an enthusiastic "Yes!"

The world has changed immensely since the first edition of the book came out in 2013. Today, boards deal with increasingly complicated issues, including remote work, the great resignation, pandemics, racial injustice, climate change, and social responsibility (Environmental, Social, and Governance, ESG). We now have more diversity in our board members, but not nearly enough.

It was immediately apparent to me, others, and most importantly to Brad, Matt, and Mahendra that the book's first edition had a significant flaw. The stories were all told from a single voice—same race, same gender, same age and thus missing the richness that the best modern boards today reflect. With a good amount of humility, Brad admitted that the book in this state wasn't acceptable, nor was it an accurate representation of startup boards. And then, Brad did what he does so well: he worked hard to change the narrative by spending extra time learning, engaging in many new conversations to expand his network, and broadening the diversity of the people whose stories were in the book. It's not easy to operationalize the intention to make diversity a reality. Extending networks requires leaders to spend the time and energy to find resources outside what they already know and isn't something that can be delegated.

This edition has more voices telling stories from different perspectives. Because of this, I hope that a broader audience will find interest in this book, its stories, and the roles of CEO, founder, investor, and board member. The future we face demands that the brightest, most passionate, and most engaged people from all backgrounds work together—not a select, similar few.

I've often heard the phrase, "You can't be what you can't see." While it's easy to think of the phrase as something applicable to role models for kids, it's equally valid for the world of business, professions, and academics. Nowhere in the corporate world are things more cloaked under a veil of secrecy than in the boardroom. Few people ever get the opportunity to "see" the inside of a boardroom or participate in a board meeting. And when conjuring up an image of a typical board member, most envision a 62-year-old White male who was previously a CEO or CFO or an investor who sits on many, perhaps too many, boards as part of an investment firm. While these are familiar images, they aren't the complete picture, and the landscape is changing. For example, you'll see a story from me in these pages. I'm a seasoned product executive who joined her first board in her forties.

Startup Boards shines at demystifying the startup boardroom. It provides readers with an insider's account of board issues, dynamics, and challenges. By breaking down exactly what a board of directors does, what a board member is, what the job entails, and all the scenarios accompanying it, many executives—of all backgrounds—can start to see themselves in this role. In addition, a new section of the book provides the details of getting that first board seat, so readers who want to have a board role can benefit.

The best companies and the most effective boards seek to gain a variety of perspectives. Guiding companies requires experiences and questions from board members representing various industries, business models, growth stages, ESG experience, customer segments, and functional expertise. One key challenge to building diverse boards is that these roles have traditionally been filled through personal networks, which are limited. Thankfully, many, including our team at Him for Her and Matt's team at Bolster (both of which Brad supports), are working to make it easier to extend networks and build better boards.

The content in this book is helpful to all in the board ecosystem. I hope it engages a broad audience as we collectively pave the path to a more diverse group of people who form and shape our boards and the companies they steward.

Jocelyn Mangan
Him for Her, founder/CEO
February 2022

Preface

The first time I saw the inside of a boardroom, I was the most junior executive at MovieFone, a public company I worked at from 1995–1999 as the "internet guy." MovieFone was an interactive telephone/media company at the dawn of the commercial internet. The board consisted of the founders, the chairman/majority shareholder (the CEO's father and a formidable character I'd met a few times), one of the chair's business associates, and one independent director (the even more formidable Strauss Zelnick).

I gave my "state of the department" presentation to that board. I found presenting to that board of directors similar to how a lawyer must experience arguing a case before the Supreme Court. You talk for two minutes, someone interrupts you with a question, and then you stand in the firing line until someone mercifully tells you that it's over. You slink out of the room, rethinking every word that just came out of your mouth, wishing you could have a do-over.

While I worked there, I presented to the MovieFone board several times. Each session was uncomfortable, but I got a lot out of each one. I constantly confronted one question, "Why is your group losing so much money?" I responded each time with an unsatisfying combination of mumbled apologies, while pointing out that other internet businesses were losing much more money.

Even though that wasn't a winning answer with the MovieFone board, it was a formative experience in my career. By the time I started my first company, Return Path, I felt like at least I had a running start on how to form, lead, and report to my board of directors.

I was CEO of Return Path and chaired its board for two decades. We scaled the business through multiple pivots, acquisitions, financings, divestitures, growth spurts, layoffs, two recessions, 9/11, and the dot-com bust. When Validity acquired Return Path in 2019, we were a vibrant, $100 million revenue, profitable industry leader.

Our board started with two independent directors and me. It grew to a highly functioning board, including three great venture capitalists (Fred Wilson, Greg Sands, and Brad Feld, coauthor of this book) and two outstanding independent directors (Scott Petry and Jeff Epstein). Over two decades, we have had over 15 directors serve on the board. I learned how to build and run an effective board of directors from each of them.

While I've made many mistakes, I've gotten a lot of things correct and have learned a lot. I realized the immense power of a strong board many times, but the most memorable was a board meeting when we were wrestling with several tough decisions since the business was going sideways. These decisions included whether to sell off two business units to focus on our most promising line of business, even though that meant shrinking the company by over 50%. We were also considering whether to expand internationally, and whether we should build an indirect sales channel. In a long and boisterous board meeting stretching from the boardroom to a dinner that included my senior management team, we charted a bold new course for the business that set us on a path we ended up following to a successful exit a dozen years later. A less functional board could have taken a more conservative approach. The business likely wouldn't have thrived and might not even have survived.

Today, my new company, Bolster, helps startups, scaleups, and public companies find and recruit talented executive leaders, mentors, and coaches. We help CEOs build their boards and have helped dozens of CEOs think strategically about bringing in independent directors. We help CEOs determine the kind of executives they want to add to their boards. And, we help them find, hire, and compensate those directors.

I've taken a different approach to building Bolster's board. The Return Path board consisted of seven White males with prior board experience, similar to most companies throughout history. In contrast, the Bolster board has two White men, one Black man, and three women, one of whom is Asian-American, one of whom is Black, and one of whom is Latina. Four of them are first-time directors. Three of our investors, who are White men, chose to be board observers rather than take a board seat so we could fill board seats with diverse directors. It's early in Bolster's life, but I already feel that our board is more powerful and effective than the one we had at Return Path, especially at this stage. This approach is a new way to scale up a board: leveraging excellence through the observer roles while expanding the boardroom's diversity of experience and demographics.

I've served on a dozen boards and chaired about half of them, including private companies, a public company, a non-profit board, university alumni boards, and a complex industry trade association board with over 40 members. I've spent a lot of time with venture capitalists and entrepreneurs understanding their views on boards. I've also observed my wife Mariquita's experience serving on and chairing several non-profit, civic, and community organization boards.

After completing the second edition of *Startup CEO: A Field Guide to Scaling Up Your Business* and the first edition of *Startup CXO: A Field Guide to Scaling Up Your Company's Critical Functions and Teams,* I realized that I often wrote and blogged about boards publicly for Bolster and on my blog at startupceo.com. I approached Brad, whom I've worked with in different capacities for 20 years (including sitting on four other boards together), and Mahendra, whom I met when he and Brad wrote the first edition of *Startup Boards: Getting the Most Out of Your Board of Directors,* about collaborating on a second edition.

Since the first edition was written in 2013, I thought an update could include more contemporary thinking about boards. For example, Delaware created Public Benefit Corporations (PBCs) in 2013, and the dialogue about stakeholder vs. shareholder capitalism has recently gained momentum.

While the discussion around diversity in the boardroom was becoming more extensive, George Floyd's tragic murder in 2020 significantly changed the dialog and the urgency around boardroom diversity. Finally, the COVID-19 pandemic impacted all aspects of business, including the boardroom. After a brief discussion, Brad and Mahendra enthusiastically supported the idea. The second edition is the result of our collaboration.

I hope you enjoy *Startup Boards: A Field Guide to Building and Leading an Effective Board of Directors.* If you are a CEO looking to build and lead an effective board, an investor thinking about how to improve some of the boards you are on, or an executive thinking about how to create a "board-ready" profile for yourself, as I did at MovieFone, we hope you find this book useful.

Matt Blumberg
Bolster, founder/CEO
February 2022

Section 1

Board Fundamentals

Chapter 1

Introduction

The word *boardroom* conjures up images of important people puffing on cigars or sipping Scotch while sitting in leather chairs in wood-paneled rooms. They talk about complex things that determine the company's future. Formality and seriousness fill the air. Big decisions are being made.

While first-time CEOs and founders often have an elevated view of the boardroom, great startup boards aren't fancy, complex, or pretentious. Instead, a startup board is usually a small group of people trying to help build your company.

We've served on hundreds of boards. A few were great, many were good, and some were terrible. When things were going smoothly, the board was congratulatory and supportive. When there were challenges, some board members helped, others panicked, and a few vanished. The tempo and interactions of these boards varied dramatically. In some cases, reality dominated the discussion, while often, it was ignored or denied.

After a particularly tedious board meeting, Brad realized that a startup board's default structure, composition, and approach were an artifact of the past, dating to how early venture-backed company boards operated over 40 years ago. Things had changed and evolved, but the dramatic shift in communication patterns and technology hadn't been incorporated into how most boards worked. As a result, Brad ran a two-year experiment where he tried different things—some successful, some not. As with every experiment, he did more of what worked, modified and killed what didn't, tried new things, and measured a lot of stuff.

The idea for the first edition of this book emerged during this experiment. We decided that in addition to describing the new startup board approach that resulted from Brad's experiment, it was essential to lay the groundwork and clearly explain how startup boards worked and how they could be most effective. Brad's board approach builds upon the traditional board of directors, so rather than throw it out, we use a highly functioning one as the basis for a new and more effective approach to a board of directors.

While the topic may feel dry, we've tried, as Brad and Jason Mendelson did in *Venture Deals: Be Smarter Than Your Lawyer and Venture Capitalist* (2019), to take a serious topic and cover it rigorously in plain English with our brand of humor. Our aim is to demystify how a board of directors works, discuss best and worst practices, and provide a set of tools for creating and managing an awesome board.

Unless you've been a startup executive who regularly attended board meetings and interacted with board members, you probably don't know what a startup board looks like, how it functions, or how it impacts a company. Even if you're a founder, you may never have served on a board of directors before, let alone built and managed one. Early in their careers, even venture capitalists often have little board experience.

You may envision a board as a collection of faceless notables, convening meetings around a large conference room table with agendas packed with legalese about corporate governance. You might view the board as a boys' club full of older men either telling the CEO what to do or supporting whatever the CEO wants because they are in the CEO's pocket while enjoying expensive board dinners and periodic boondoggles to exotic locations.

We wrote this book to dispel these myths, demystify the workings of a board, help you understand how to create and build your board while sharing our decades of experience about leveraging your board so it becomes a strategic asset for you and your company.

What's New in the Second Edition

Brad and Mahendra have collaborated with Matt Blumberg on this edition. You met Matt in the Preface, and we quoted him several times from his book *Startup CEO* (Blumberg, 2020) in the first edition of this book.

It's been almost a decade since we first wrote this book. Since then, a Cambrian explosion of entrepreneurial activity has occurred worldwide. We've helped democratize entrepreneurship globally through Techstars, our investments, organizations building startup communities in many different cities, and our writing. While Brad updated several of his earlier books, such as *Venture Deals* and *Startup Communities: Building an Entrepreneurial Ecosystem in Your City* (Feld, 2020), the original version of *Startup Boards* was starting to feel stale.

After completing *Startup CXO*, Matt reached out to Brad and Mahendra with ideas on revising and updating *Startup Boards*. Matt's newest company, Bolster, took over the Startup Revolution series of books and startuprev.com. Brad and Matt have served together on four boards over the past 20 years, including Matt's company (Return Path), two boards where Brad was an investor and Matt was an independent director (FeedBurner and Moz), and one non-profit that Matt co-founded and where Brad served as an independent director (Path Forward). This shared experience made it easy to collaborate on the second edition.

We've updated the content from the first edition and added more depth for first-time founders about how to build a board, recruit board members, and onboard, compensate, and evaluate them. We've added content for aspiring board directors about identifying board opportunities and preparing for their first board role. We'll extensively discuss recruiting board members, managing an advisory board, and communicating with a board. We've updated many of the book's sections, bringing in relevant research, current best practices, guidance, and learning from the changes brought to boards by the COVID-19 pandemic.

When we wrote the first edition, we had a short section on board diversity with a primary focus on gender. Over the past decade, especially in the last few years, board diversity has become a major issue in entrepreneurship. Increasing board diversity is an important goal of many entrepreneurs, investors, and entrepreneurial support organizations. This edition addresses how startups can increase board diversity and the tangible benefits of board diversity to a company.

We've added quantitative data on key startup board characteristics. Bolster created a first-of-its-kind Board Benchmark Survey as part of its larger offering of helping startups create boards.

Until Bolster's survey, the actual demographics of a board—the composition, number of directors, compensation, length of service, and several other board characteristics—were largely unknown.

Who This Book Is For

We're deeply committed to entrepreneurship, having spent our entire careers starting, funding, and building companies while helping create entrepreneurial ecosystems worldwide. Our focus on entrepreneurship, along with the book's title, may lead you to think *Startup Boards* applies only to entrepreneurs and early-stage boards.

While startup boards do have specific issues and challenges, there are far more similarities than differences. The leader of any type of organization with a board, including a larger private company, non-profit, public company, community organization, or family-owned business, will find many useful ideas in this book.

Our primary audience is founders, entrepreneurs, or non-founder CEOs. However, this book also addresses anyone on a board, including investors and outside directors. We've worked with thousands of board members, covering a wide range of experiences, challenges, and problems. While some of these board members were spectacular and had a dramatic positive impact on the trajectory and outcome of a company, many were average and had a neutral or insignificant impact. Others were detrimental, causing more problems that negatively impacted the company and the board's functioning. We've learned extensively from these experiences, which we've tried to incorporate into this book in a way that's helpful to any board member.

We also wrote this book for management teams. Most management teams are directly exposed to the board and interact with them regularly. Some participate in most board meetings, while others are called in to provide an update or explain a situation. Bringing management team members into a board meeting can be extremely helpful or completely disruptive. The responsibility for an effective relationship between board members and management team members belongs to the board members, the CEO, and the management team alike.

Finally, we include specific advice and guidance for an aspiring board member. Serving on a board is a meaningful career objective, but the challenge of getting on your first board is non-trivial. In addition to learning how to function effectively on a board, we help you learn how to be a compelling prospective board member.

Throughout this book, we've incorporated advice and stories from investors, board members, entrepreneurs, and executives whose views we respect. While we provide guidance and tools, we continuously learn, so follow our blogs and the startuprev.com website for things we have learned, new experiences, and experiments.

Magic Words, Phrases, Abbreviations, and Style

Having written several books, we've learned the importance of being precise with particular words and phrases. The following are several magic words with their synonyms and abbreviations.

Angels: We include "friends and family" and "seed" investors in the definition of an "angel investor" and shorten the phrase to "angels." These are early investors in a company who are investing their own money. We don't include "seed-stage venture capitalists" in this category.

Board: We'll start abbreviating "board of directors" as "board."

Board member, director: We use these words interchangeably.

CEO: The CEO can be one of the founders, but it doesn't have to be. Occasionally we'll refer to "*founder/CEO*" when this is an important distinction.

Chair: While "chairman of the board" sounds serious and weighty, there are plenty of "chairwomen." We prefer to use "chair" since it's gender-neutral. While in some sections we refer to a lead director, they play a similar role to a chair.

Entrepreneur, founder: We use these two words interchangeably. To us, they mean the same thing.

Lawyer, outside counsel: While we use these words interchangeably, we generally refer to outside counsel. If we refer to a lawyer who works for the company rather than an independent law firm, we'll call them "general counsel."

VC, investor: We abbreviate "venture capitalist" as "VC" and are referring to a person, not an entire firm (which we call a "VC firm"). It also takes the letter count down significantly. We also use *VC* and *investor* interchangeably.

After much debate and discussion with other writers and editors, we decided to use the Singular *they*[1] as our primary pronoun, unless we referred to a specific person.

One of the challenges with this book is writing it for a broad range of readers, including founder/CEO, non-founder CEO, VCs, the management team, independent board members, and aspiring independent directors. To avoid confusion, we address the advice in the book to the CEO, except for Section Six. When we discuss situations that only apply to a founder/CEO, we clarify that. Regardless of who the reader is, we refer to a CEO when saying "You."

Whenever we have a list of things to explain to support a point, rather than weaving seven paragraphs into the text with lots of transitional phrases, we start each paragraph with a bold bulleted summary of the point we are making. Having read 17,325 business books, we wish more authors would use this approach to make it easier to summarize and skim key points on a topic.

Whenever we refer to another person in the book, we'll include their credentials in parentheses the first time we mention them. In later references, we only list their name.

We've written this book together. While we each had different experiences, we felt using one voice would be more effective. We'll often refer to one of us in the third person. You're familiar with this approach if you've read the book *Startup Life: Surviving and Thriving in a Relationship with an Entrepreneur* (2013) that Brad wrote with his wife, Amy Batchelor.

Okay, let's begin.

Note

1. See Khan Academy's excellent presentation on this at https://www.youtube.com/watch?v=f21t7DRKlg8. Wikipedia has an extensive discussion at https://en.wikipedia.org/wiki/Singular_they. And the American Psychological Association (APA) Style guide has a clear explanation at https://apastyle.apa.org/style-grammar-guidelines/grammar/singular-they.

Chapter 2

The Board's Purpose

Why have a board of directors in the first place? What do they do? How big should they be? Do you even need one?

A board is legally required the day you incorporate your company. Frequently, the board consists of the founders, or even just one founder, until a startup receives outside financing.

Waiting to build a board is a mistake.

Your board can be a powerful strategic asset. If you choose the right directors, build and manage your board effectively, and actively engage your directors, the board can help you dramatically accelerate your business. When you run into trouble, which all startups inevitably do, the board can help guide you through the tough spots. As Jeff Lawson of Twilio is fond of saying, "As the founder and CEO, I get to build two teams to help me—my leadership team and my board."

Clint Korver (Ulu Ventures, Partner), who used to teach a course at Stanford University titled "Startup Boards: Advanced Entrepreneurship," says, "The most common mistake startups make is not having a board at all." Clint points out that research shows that most startups fail due to self-inflicted wounds, including internal decisions about founding team roles and equity allocations. "Founders who are overconfident or choose to avoid conflict often miss an opportunity to bring in fresh perspective with input from appropriate individuals," says Clint.

Depending upon the stage of the company, three kinds of boards exist: (1) a working board; (2) a reporting board; or (3) a lame-duck board. Ideally, for a startup, a working board is best as the board members don't pontificate, ask mindless questions or just show up for meetings relatively uninformed. Instead, they focus on the critical challenges of a company.

Accountability

In *Startup CEO* (2020), Matt wrote that the fundamental reason boards exist is that "everybody needs a boss." For many founders, one of the reasons to create a startup is to get away from having a boss. Unless you own 100% of your startup, are a solo founder, have no intentions to ever grant or sell equity to anyone, and don't think you benefit from anyone else's experience and knowledge, you're accountable to others. Even then, you're still accountable to stakeholders, including employees, vendors, and customers.

The board ensures that the interests of all shareholders and other stakeholders are considered. In many startups, the primary shareholders and board members are the same. As companies grow, outside board members who aren't involved in the business and don't have a significant economic stake are added to the board. Collectively, this group is responsible for considering and balancing the interests of all shareholders.

Accountability is a powerful construct. Consider how effective you are at dieting or exercising on your own. Are you more effective if you have a nutritionist, trainer, coach, or friend to whom you're accountable? Regardless of how much you enjoyed your favorite class in college, how many papers would you have written if your professor hadn't assigned them and given them due dates? While it's possible to be completely self-taught and highly disciplined in elements of your life, it's rare to maximize your success without help, support, and accountability.

General Responsibilities

A board has other vital roles beyond holding the CEO and team accountable.

- **Organize Your Thinking:** With company communication running on email, Slack, text messaging, and numerous other applications, the quality of communication deteriorates, especially around significant decisions. Scribbled bullet points or half-baked spreadsheets enter the communication flow between team members. Long memos, overwrought internal wikis, or endless PowerPoint presentations waste enormous time, slow down decision-making, and become a crutch for critical thinking. A board forces your team to think through and question all aspects of what they are presenting, consolidate the communication, and commit to decisions.

- **Match Patterns:** An experienced board member links their historical experience to your current situation. They'll see a chain of events unfolding, reflect on something they experienced at another company, or identify a dangerous path you are heading down. The board member provides content, advice, and introductions to other founders or CEOs who have had a similar issue and can be a resource for you. While the board member might not have answers to every situation, it creates more context to help you steer your company around icebergs and avoid the damage lurking beneath the surface. The wonderful aphorism often attributed to Mark Twain, "History doesn't repeat itself, but it often rhymes," applies.

- **See the Forest for the Trees:** You're close to your business and in the weeds of day-to-day activity. Your board isn't. A board member can point out things you completely miss, especially when mired in your operating results, team dynamics, or performance. While the board member can help you one-on-one, the collective board creates space for you and your leadership team to periodically engage in a higher-level discussion about the business.

- **Drive Intellectually Honest Discussion and Debate:** Even strong executive teams have difficulty disagreeing with a dominant CEO. The vast majority of boards don't. A healthy board challenges you and your team's assumptions while demonstrating how to engage in honest debate to get to an answer.

- **Create a Forcing Function for Deadlines and Quality:**
  A board creates a cadence for running your company
  around a set of regular, recurring deadlines. Unless you're
  in a business that has significant external deadlines imposed
  on it by partners or customers, deadlines often become elusive, regularly slip, or become vague targets, as in "next
  week," "next month," or "later this year." While many deadlines are arbitrary, a lack of accountability can lead to pro-
  crastination and excuses. A public commitment to a
  deadline is powerful. While you may not reach it, decide to
  change it, or prioritize other activities, you'll have a board
  to keep you accountable.
- **Support Transactional Activity:** A CEO shouldn't negotiate a round of financing, the sale of the company, or an
  acquisition of another company alone. Many board members have more negotiating experience than the CEO and
  should be resources for helping improve a deal. Savvy VCs
  may know which investor groups make good partners and
  which ones to avoid. Finally, the board can veto any decision a CEO may have made if the board perceives the
  decision not to be in the company's best interests.

The CEO reports to the board. However, the board doesn't
run the company—the CEO does. A common refrain of Brad's is,
"My most important decision as a board member is whether I support the CEO. My job is to do everything I know to help the CEO
succeed. If I don't, it's my job to work with the CEO and the board
to get back to where I support the CEO. Ultimately, if the board
loses confidence in the CEO, it's our job to replace the CEO."
Effective board members understand the nuance between supporting the CEO and having the CEO report to them.

Chapter 3

Legal Characteristics

A board is a legal construct with a well-defined set of requirements and responsibilities that fall under the term "corporate governance." The board's formal duties include the legal concepts of *duty of care* and *duty of loyalty*. Boards also have smaller working groups, including audit, compensation, and nominating committees. While startup boards should be agile, it's useful to understand the formal requirements.

As a startup grows, the number of stakeholders increases. In the beginning, a startup has a small team, often just the founders. A few early employees are added and given stock options. The company raises a small amount of money, adding a few angel investors and possibly a VC. The company releases its product, gaining customers and suppliers who become stakeholders in the startup. More employees are added, and, if it's a venture-backed company, the company raises a VC round. Soon, you'll have a lot of divergent interests among the stakeholders. The board is ultimately responsible for navigating any conflicts that arise.

It's essential to put a structure in place early to ensure the board and leadership team minimize conflicts of interest and understand how to navigate them. Good boards invite counsel to participate in meetings to help the company follow best practices. While entrepreneurs are rightfully concerned about racking up legal fees in such situations, Eric Jensen (Cooley, Partner) states, "Just as a VC is focused on building the company using best practices, a good attorney does not focus just on legal aspects. We act as advisors first, sitting in board meetings for free and alerting the CEO to any warning signs we spot in these board meetings."

A Board Member's Legal Duties

The state laws in which the company is incorporated, and the company's charter documents (the Articles of Incorporation and Bylaws) establish the legal duties of a board member. Federal securities laws and the Securities and Exchange Commission (SEC) add bonus rules for public companies.

A *fiduciary duty* is an obligation to act in the best interest of another party and is the highest standard of care the law can impose on someone. A fiduciary is expected to be completely loyal to the person or entity they owe the duty, who is also called the "principal." Specifically, the fiduciary mustn't put their interests before the interests of the principal and must not profit from their position as a fiduciary unless the principal consents. Every board member has a fiduciary duty to the shareholders unless the company is a Public Benefit Corporation (PBC), where, under Delaware law, the fiduciary duty is to the stakeholders as defined in the company's charter.

My attitude when I'm on a board is to be supportive of management teams, to be a sounding board, and to offer constructive criticism at times. The board shares the responsibility to the company and the shareholders and we're not just cheerleaders—there are legal and fiduciary responsibilities that are often cut-and-dried. For instance, our board was contacted by an employee who said, "I'm quitting, and I want you to know that some of the numbers that you're being shown at the board meetings aren't really accurate." As a board we need to get to the truth of that; is it a parting shot from a disgruntled employee or do we have a management team that isn't representing things accurately? We hired an internal audit firm to look at the books and tried to understand how it added up to what we were being shown. It turned out that the numbers were accurate, but that situation was cut-and-dried: we were given information that we had to investigate.

Legal and fiduciary responsibilities to me are in some ways easy, but the more difficult decisions for a board are the ones that are not legal or fiduciary, but ethically important. For example, we had a member of a firm where we were investors post comments that were homophobic on Twitter. That's not a legal or fiduciary issue, but we asked if we could coach that person. Being on a board is more than legal and fiduciary responsibilities but also involves ethical responsibilities. You need to make sure that the right thing happens.

Rebecca Kaden, Union Square Ventures, Partner

The *duty of care* and the *duty of loyalty* primarily define board members' fiduciary duties.

- **Duty of Care:** A board member needs to be attentive and prudent in making board-level decisions, acting in good faith, and conducting enough business investigation and supervision to provide an informed basis for decisions. A board member breaches their duty of care when they act negligently or know that the consequences of an action could be harmful to the company.
- **Duty of Loyalty:** A board member should ensure that the company's interests are always on their mind. Loyalty to the company supersedes any other vested interests the board member might have. A board member breaches their duty of loyalty when they put their interests ahead of the company, conduct inappropriate transactions which benefit the board member ("self-dealing"), or benefit personally from confidential information shared in the boardroom.

VC board members, especially when they are major shareholders, are also focused on making a financial return for their fund, which can generate a conflict of interest in certain situations. Jon Callaghan (True Ventures, Managing Partner) says, "As long as you are a board member, you have to focus on what is best for all shareholders. This can be difficult for VCs. Afterward, you can go home and fret all you want about your fund not making a better return." In actual conflict situations, a VC should explain the conflict and either recuse themselves or honor their fiduciary duty to the company in a board vote, while reserving the right to vote differently as a shareholder.

Additional legal obligations include the *duty of confidentiality* and the *duty of disclosure*. While linked to the duty of care and duty of loyalty, they're just as important.

- **Duty of Confidentiality:** A subset of the duty of loyalty, the duty of confidentiality requires a board member to maintain the confidentiality of nonpublic information about the company.

- **Duty of Disclosure:** A subset of both the duties of care and loyalty, the duty of disclosure requires a board member to take reasonable steps to ensure that a company provides its stockholders with all material information about a matter for which stockholder action is sought.

While these duties may sound conceptually straightforward, in practice, they're subject to judgment and interpretation based on the specific situation. In legal disputes over board action, courts apply a legal construct, called the *business judgment rule*, which gives deference to the decisions of boards where the directors acted in good faith and in an informed manner. Courts generally apply the business judgment rule and uphold the decisions of boards if:

a. The directors don't have any personal interest in the outcome.
b. The directors have reviewed all relevant information before deciding.
c. The directors believe that the decision is in the best interests of the company.

This rule helps protect a director from personal liability for bad business decisions by essentially shifting the burden of proof to a plaintiff to demonstrate that the director didn't satisfy this test. On the other hand, if directors have an interest in the decision or fail to adequately inform themselves about the decision to be made, courts may apply a more rigorous standard to the board's conduct.

Addressing Conflicting Duties

Conflicts between fiduciary duties, such as the one mentioned by Jon Callaghan above, periodically come up in the boardroom. Some VCs are transparent when faced with a conflict, while others are opaque. In other situations, especially with inexperienced VCs, they aren't even aware of the conflict. Helping you identify and navigate these situations is another reason to have experienced outside counsel at every board meeting.

If you get your knowledge and experience about boardroom dynamics from TV shows like *Billions* and *Succession,* you might think that the legal dynamics are the things the lawyers have to deal with, so your goal is just to win the negotiation when there's a conflict. However, if you are trying to build an effective company with a highly functional board, you'll realize that whenever a conflict arises, the best approach is to air it out, debate it, and figure out a solution before the conflict escalates.

Imagine a situation where an acquirer makes a moderately appealing offer to buy a company. In this situation, the founders, the common shareholders, the early investors (let's call them Early VC), and the employees will make a nice return. However, the last-round investor will only get its money back. While the company can continue to operate for a year with the cash in the bank, the founders and early investors decide they would like to sell the company. However, the last-round investor (let's call the firm Late VC) doesn't want to sell.

Late VC previously negotiated blocking rights as part of its protective provisions (in the financing documents) on the sale of a company for less than 1.5× their investment. This disagreement is the first time this particular issue has come up, and no one other than the Late VC realizes that Late VC can block the transaction using its protective provision.

The board discusses the transaction extensively, with Late VC insisting the company should keep running independently for at least another year, given the potential future opportunity. However, the founders and Early VC want to cash in. Not realizing that Late VC has blocking rights, Early VC says, "Let's put it to a vote." The founder/CEO forgot to invite outside counsel to the board meeting, so no one reminds the board members of Late VC's blocking rights.

In this situation, there's a board vote and, while Late VC votes against the transaction, a majority of board members vote to sell the company. However, Late VC says, "Hang on a second, I'm going to exercise my preferred right to block the sale of the company." Everyone looks at each other angrily. Early VC rolls out the phrase "fiduciary duty" and angrily tries to school Late VC, who is very experienced, that Late VC has a fiduciary duty to all share-holders. Late VC smiles coyly and counters that it also has a fiduci-ary duty to its limited partners and is protecting that duty by exercising the protective provision it negotiated as part of the last financing round.

Eventually, one of the founders says, "Late VC board member, what do you want?"

Late VC responds, "At least 1.5× my investment or let's keep running the company since we have plenty of cash on the balance sheet—the cash that I recently gave you!"

It's worth recognizing the Late VC could have also voted, in its capacity as a board member, for the transaction but then exer-cised its protective provision separately to block the transaction from proceeding.

There are multiple solutions to this situation. But understand-ing the potential conflicts early, especially in any transactional situations, and having open discussions about how to resolve them that include the advice of counsel are the best approach.

Benefit Corporations and the B Corp Movement

Until recently, U.S. corporate law wasn't structured to address the situation of for-profit companies that wanted to pursue a social or environmental mission. While corporations generally can pursue a broad range of activities, corporate decision-making is justified through creating long-term shareholder value.

Benefit corporations, often called Public Benefit Corporations (PBCs) because of the Delaware legal framework, expand the fiduciary duty of directors to require them to consider non-financial stakeholders and shareholders, creating legal protec-tion for directors and officers to consider additional stakeholders. Currently, 35 states and the District of Columbia include state laws for benefit corporations.

Benefit corporations don't differ much from traditional C corporations. Changing to a Benefit Corp from a C Corp is straightforward and simply requires a change to the corporate bylaws. While third-party certification isn't required, many com-panies choose to be certified by the non-profit B Lab to meet rigorous social and environmental performance standards, accountability, and transparency. Brad's VC Firm, Foundry, became a B Corp in 2016 and has been a B Corp advocate since then.[1]

At the core of the B Corp movement is the idea that all companies share a duty to build responsible businesses for their employees, customers, and communities. There's a current view that businesses that treat their constituents well can attract and retain employees better, innovate faster, grow more quickly, and create more value. Additionally, some entrepreneurs assert that they are trying to create a better world through the daily actions taken by their businesses. By integrating responsible practices throughout an organization, companies can build better businesses while at the same time being agents for positive change.

While B Corps require a different philosophy of governance than LLCs or C Corps, the board's general role and attributes are similar. Consequently, the fundamentals of building and leading a board of directors remain the same.

Should You Get D&O Insurance?

In conducting board duties, numerous decisions have to be made. Directors aim to function with transparency and conduct their affairs in the most diligent manner, yet certain outcomes can lead to lawsuits. It's an occupational hazard.

Issues may arise from existing shareholders who believe that the directors didn't act in the interest of all shareholders or get appropriate approvals. In certain situations where the corporation fails to meet its federal or state obligations, such as taxes, environmental safety, or occupational health, the government can initiate action against the corporation. Former employees can sue directors for a variety of reasons.

Corporations indemnify their directors and officers through their bylaws and indemnification agreements with individual directors. Indemnification is the first line of defense for both your board of directors and your officers. Indemnification includes expenses (including attorney's fees), judgments, fines, settlements, and other amounts reasonably incurred with any proceeding, arising because such person is or was an agent of the corporation.

However, startups are generally cash-constrained, and any legal action will impact already scarce cash resources. As a result, the second line of defense is a solid D&O (directors and officers) insurance policy. Such a policy helps preserve corporate funds. In certain situations, corporations become insolvent and yet have lawsuits lingering on. D&O insurance becomes the only source of your legal defense funds in these situations.

D&O insurance offers protection to the board of directors and the corporation's officers. Insurance pays for defense costs and can cover some or all damages. Early-stage (pre-revenue/ product development) startups should aim to procure between $1 million and $3 million in coverage, typically costing $5,000– $10,000 per year. As the company matures, these amounts should be revisited and increased for the actual size of the company and current market norms.

D&O policies will have several variables, including the scope of coverage, the annual premium, deductibles, limits on the maximum amount covered, and the term of coverage. As with any insurance policy, you should negotiate carefully with several vendors. At the minimum, make sure you understand what the policy covers concerning the following:

- Director and officer wrongdoings within specific terms. The policy definition of "wrongful acts" needs to be understood clearly by each director. Fraud or criminal conduct may be obvious. On the other hand, negligent acts or "intentional harm" can fall into the subjective category. Also, the insurance should cover directors from the actions of other directors or officers. Minor changes in policy language can have a significant impact on costs.
- The cost of indemnifying directors and officers.
- Defense costs only or defense and damages? Watch for limits and exclusions. The broader the coverage combined with limited exclusions translates to a high premium.
- Exclusions state things not covered by the insurance policy. These can include misconduct, blatant fraudulent acts,

willful breaches of laws, or criminal conduct. Also, certain exclusions can eliminate coverage when one director sues another, or the corporation sues the director.

- Selection of counsel: In some policies, the D&O insurance company has the right to select defense counsel, similar to your car insurance company picking the shop that can repair your car when you have an accident.
- The process of filing claims, approving defense expenses, or conditions of denial of coverage need to be understood clearly.
- Ensure that the corporation's *general liability coverage* insurance policy does not duplicate the coverage with the D&O policy. It's easy to get overinsured and pay too much when your insurance broker is eager and not acting in your best interest.

An insurance broker will identify the insurance provider and offer a quote. Your board should be actively involved in studying the various options and the selection of an insurance carrier. Don't change coverage or let the policy lapse without input from your board.

Note

1. Seth Levine, "Joining the B Team," *VC Adventure,* May 18, 2016. https://www.sethlevine.com/archives/2016/05/joining-the-b -team.html (accessed January 17, 2022).

Chapter 4

Board Member Roles

A board without defined roles will never be as effective as one that has defined roles, even in its simplest structure. There are different ways to assign roles to directors and rotate them through these roles. Being clear about roles and expectations is critical, so board members know their responsibilities.

Chair or Lead Director

Boards need a leader. Historically, this role has been titled "chairman," although we prefer to shorten it simply to "chair." More recently, as the debate over the split between chair and CEO has intensified, a new construct, a "lead director," has emerged. For most purposes, "chairman," "chair," and "lead director" are interchangeable.

While a founder or the CEO is often also the chair of the board, there are plenty of situations where you want a board chair to be different from the founder or CEO. For some investors, this is a requirement for them to invest.

If your lead investor has experience as a board chair, that's often a good solution. However, many VC investors have no experience as a board chair, lack an understanding of the role of a board chair, or have a history of overplaying their role as board chair. You may run into the VC or potential board member who says, "I'll only serve on your board if I can be the chair." Be wary of this and do your diligence into the person as a potential board chair.

A board chair's role differs from that of the other board members and requires subtle and deft interpersonal skills. The following are characteristics of a good board chair:

- **Ensures Alignment:** The board exists to help the company be successful. But definitions of success vary. A good chair keeps an eye on the big picture and ensures each meeting is a step in the right direction by working with the CEO on the meeting agenda. When someone gets off track, derails a meeting, has a divergent agenda, or causes other random disruptions, the board chair refocuses the board meeting.
- **Is a Good Facilitator:** The board meeting is where information is shared and decisions are made. People want to be heard, yet loud voices often drown out quieter ones. Some board members focus on showing how smart they are, while others lock horns around trivial issues. A good chair allows all voices to be heard, draws out the quieter participants, and gets all the relevant information on the table while driving the discussion to a decision.
- **Is a Proactive Communicator:** A good chair manages all one-on-one communications proactively with the CEO. While any board member can choose to mentor and guide the CEO, the chair has special responsibility for synthesizing all of the feedback and delivering it to the CEO consistently.
- **Helps the CEO Set the Board Agenda:** While the CEO will set the agenda for each board meeting, the chair helps by collecting feedback from other directors about what they want to cover. The chair then helps the CEO create an agenda that will effectively engage board members in a vibrant discussion.
- **Manages the Clock:** Board members are busy people with significant and conflicting demands on their time. It's essential to begin and end the meeting on time, conforming to a predefined agenda and moving the conversation along when it stalls.

- **Maintains Culture and Hygiene:** As an advocate for the company, the chair creates and maintains a positive and constructive culture, especially in times of challenge and stress. Wasting time, allowing a hostile dynamic between board members to become the norm, alienating individual board members, or overemphasizing individual flaws are not helpful.
- **Helps the CEO Process Board Feedback:** The chair is responsible for gathering feedback from other directors by taking notes in Executive and Closed Sessions and spending time with the CEO after the meeting to debrief that feedback.

Following are some thoughts from Karen DeGolia (Vontier, Board Chair), who has been a chair or lead director multiple times.

The role of a lead director is to make sure that the board is completing its work of governance, making sure the agenda properly reflects what the company needs to communicate or get approval for, as well as what the directors want to know. It also involves working with the CEO to make sure that the interaction between the CEO and the company is effective, helpful, and productive for all parties.

The lead director often becomes a very trusted confidant for the CEO, which is somewhat of a lonely job. As CEO you can't really confide in most of your direct reports on every topic and the chair or lead director is the person that you can confide in. It's really important for the CEO and lead director to have a great interpersonal relationship that allows that CEO to actually be vulnerable and share what they think is working well or isn't. The lead director can collaborate to find good solutions to assist the CEO in their work.

An effective lead director needs to have excellent EQ (emotional quotient) because you need to be able to understand where the different parties (directors or management) are coming from and help work through discussions to resolve issues in a way that makes everyone feel that they've been heard and that all elements were considered. It's important to understand where people are coming from and make them feel that the time that they commit to is productive and valued. That takes a fair amount of listening and humility.

Finally, a good lead director realizes that it's not about them. In order to be successful, the lead director should walk into a room with a team, rather than a power, mindset.

Karen DeGolia, Vontier, Board Chair

Executive Chair

The executive chair is a chair who is an active member of the management team rather than an outside director. Often the executive chair is a founder of the company and can often be the largest non-investor shareholder in the business. It can also be a founder who was previously the CEO but has handed that role to another founder or hired someone to be the CEO. An executive chair can be a full-time or part-time employee of the company, but in either case, has a significant role in some aspect of the company.

Few people have been as successful as Reid Hoffman as executive chair. Reid co-founded LinkedIn and is also a partner at the VC firm Greylock, a significant investor in LinkedIn before Microsoft acquired it. Here, Reid explains how he approaches the role of executive chair (which officially was "Executive Chairman" while he was at LinkedIn).

A few years after I co-founded LinkedIn in 2003, I decided to shift my role from CEO to executive chairman. While there are a relatively clear-cut set of roles and responsibilities attached to the CEO's job, an executive chairman at company X may play a much different role than the executive chair at company Y. It's a nebulous job title and depends on the company in question and the person filling the role.

I made the shift because LinkedIn was in a state of transition, shifting from a startup to a growth-stage company. I love articulating a product vision and other facets of early-stage entrepreneurship, but I'm less interested in organization building, international expansion, and developing scalable business processes. Becoming executive chairman allowed me to continue playing a highly active role at LinkedIn regarding strategy and several key projects while handing off the operations to the CEO.

Jeff Weiner became CEO in 2009, and, while I remained extremely involved at LinkedIn, the division of responsibilities between us was extremely clear. The buck stopped with Jeff. If Jeff made a decision, that decision was made. Period. While I tried to offer Jeff honest and candid advice and even challenged him, he had operational control over the company. Jeff worked for the company, not for the executive chairman or the board, although the board could choose to replace him.

Trust is the critical factor in an executive chairman and CEO relationship. Neither works explicitly for the other, and no one reported to me. I was careful never to override the organizational chain of command.

My most important job as executive chairman was helping Jeff do the best job possible. Sometimes this meant helping recruit and retain great people. Sometimes this meant helping launch an international expansion or a new product. It always meant being a great partner to Jeff and the entire executive team so that we could advance our vision of bringing economic opportunity to every professional in the global workforce with our thousands of LinkedIn colleagues around the world.

Reid Hoffman, Greylock Partner, LinkedIn Founder, and Executive Chairman until the sale to Microsoft

Should You Be Chair of Your Board?

Until the Enron scandal and the ensuing Sarbanes-Oxley legislation in the early 2000s, almost all US-based CEOs were board chairs of their company. Today, 75% of public companies in the United States are still set up that way, although there is a growing movement to separate CEO and chair roles. There are good reasons for that, with larger, public companies and private companies with long and checkered pasts rife with governance issues. It's also common for nonprofits and associations with different stakeholder structures to separate the CEO and board chair roles. However, in closely held private companies, it probably doesn't matter much.

If your board or a major investor insists on someone else being chair, you can always push back and suggest appointing a "lead independent director" instead. If you are a CEO at this type of company, having a lead director or not being the board's chair primarily means two things:

1. You still run the meetings and write all the materials since you run the business.
2. You have one person to consult with on the meeting agenda and the materials ahead of time.

Matt (the founder/entrepreneur) prefers combining the CEO and chair role as the overall leader of the company for a private company, but he can see both arguments. In contrast, while Brad (the VC) is fine with the combined CEO/chair role, he prefers a CEO + lead director role in private companies, especially at later stages.

Independent Board Members

Most board members in a startup represent either the investors or the founders. An independent board member represents neither group. Optimally, an independent board member will be unbiased and ultimately concerned about the company and its shareholders and stakeholders rather than the specific interests of an investor or a founder. The composition of a startup board is often specified in the company's governing documents to create a balance between investors and founders with at least one independent board member.

Data show that in venture-backed companies, board control is typically split between investors and founders more than 60% of the time, with an independent third-party director holding the tie-breaking vote.[1] If the independent director is well respected and has the trust of both the investor and founder board members, they can often act as a mediator or voice of reason when conflict arises. Jocelyn Mangan, whom you met in the Foreword, says, "One of the worst things in a company or a board is groupthink. In a world where a board needs to see around corners and make tough decisions, the voices in the conversation must come from different experiences. When the board is a founder and only investors, adding independent directors offers the opportunity to round out the conversation with the unique perspective of an operator, which in many cases is even more relevant than the heavily weighted financial perspective."

Founders and investors should invest the time and effort to identify the right independent board members and bring them in as quickly as possible. Unfortunately, this effort is frequently deferred, often to the company's detriment. While financing documents often provide for an independent director as part of the board, this seat is often left empty due to the excitement of the new investment, the pressure to get the product out, the intensity of the work of scaling the company, or the lack of appreciation of the value of an outside director.

Board Observers

Many boards have *board observers* who have the right to sit in, observe, and participate in portions of the board meeting but don't have formal board roles or responsibilities. Observers don't get to vote on board matters, and are often VCs or co-founders of the company.

To limit the size of a board, many companies grant observer seats to investors. In other cases, strategic investors get observer rights instead of actual board seats to limit their control. Some strategic investors prefer board observer status, as it minimizes any liabilities their corporation may face due to actions of the board and individual board members.

VC partners who want a junior member of their firm to participate in board meetings often also ask for an observer right in addition to a board seat. In the best case, these junior members of the firm don't show up without the VC board member partner and never end up being a "proxy board member" for the actual board member. Instead, they're observers. They listen to what is going on, help support their VC partner when appropriate, and only weigh into the discussion when they have something significant from their experience to add.

Early in the life of a company, more than one founder may be on the board. As the board grows, the number of founders on the board is often reduced. While there can be a founder seat and a CEO seat, the CEO may no longer be a founder or additional founders may have observer rights.

Observers don't have a right to be in the board's executive session or closed session. Observers will respect this, but it can be taken to a ridiculous level, where there are essentially two separate board meetings. With the observers in attendance, the first one ends up being a high-level reporting session. The actual board meeting follows this, attended only by board members, where the material is again reviewed, but this time with substantive discussion. If you're going to give someone an observer seat, you should expect that they'll be in all but the most sensitive conversations.

While an entrepreneur may think they are managing the size of their board through using observer rights, we've sat in boardrooms with 20 people or more, where only five of them were board members. We've experienced VC firms who use their observer rights to "bring power to the board meeting." Instead of one board seat, the observer seat is used to effectively have two board members. And we've been in situations where it's confusing who is a board member and who isn't.

Ultimately, it's the lead director and the CEO's responsibility to manage the observer dynamic. Creating a clear set of rules and expectations and living by them are the best way to manage and get value from board observers.

Outside Counsel

A capable lawyer from a law firm who understands startups, which we'll refer to throughout this book as outside counsel, is a powerful addition to the boardroom. While they rarely take a board seat, you should include them in all board activities. If your company is large enough to have a general counsel on your management team, you should include them in all board meetings and board activities.

Experienced outside counsel understands their role well and should give you satisfying answers to the following questions.

- Will they attend all board meetings for free or at a discounted rate?
- Will they maintain all corporate records?
- Whom do they represent—the company, the board, investors, or the CEO?
- Will they advise the CEO on relevant matters in managing the dynamic between the board, investors, and the CEO?
- Will they advise the board on governance matters, especially where the board and their financial interests as investors diverge?
- Will they participate in an annual board performance review?

Your outside counsel isn't just there to focus and pay attention to "legal stuff." Following are some thoughts from Mike Platt (Cooley, Partner) on the role a lawyer can play in a company's growth.

Outside counsel plays a significant role in helping a young company grow through an IPO or an exit. Providing good legal advice is table stakes. Startup lawyers need to be business-minded, recognizing that early-stage companies must remain nimble and take considerable business risks. This shouldn't be confused with ignoring legal issues, but rather having these issues be thoughtfully discussed.

An outside counsel earns their keep by helping boards and companies with creative, and hopefully simple, solutions to complex business issues. To accomplish this, outside counsel needs the support of good board members, access to decision-makers, and involvement early in the decision-making process. If you worry that bringing your lawyer in too early will be expensive, you have the wrong lawyer.

The following are objectives a CEO and board members should expect from outside counsel.

- *Represent the Company and Stockholders*: Counsel must provide a neutral and dispassionate perspective regarding legal matters and transactions. In many venture-backed companies, outside counsel is often the only person in the boardroom without a material financial interest in the company. Transactions often have conflicting interests between classes of stock, investors with different liquidity time horizons, and management vs. investment interests. Outside counsel facilitates open discussion of potential conflicts and helps structure transactions that maximize alignment while being explicit about conflicts.
- *Participate Appropriately in Board Meetings*: Board meetings are a time for developing strategy and, except in the most material transactions, not for analyzing detailed and nuanced legal risks. The responsibility for keeping the dialogue at the strategy level lies with both outside counsel and the board. While outside counsel can be the guilty party for hijacking the agenda, board members often suggest concerns with "legal issues" to avoid conflict with management on more fundamental business concerns. If outside counsel is at the board meeting, they can help dismiss these attempts to avoid real issues.
- *Engage with Management and the Board Collectively and Independently*: Outside counsel should build relationships with the board and management. The CEO should encourage and facilitate these relationships. Non-management board members should demand direct access to counsel and be responsive to outside counsel's requests for engagement with them on matters, especially those involving management conflicts of interest.
- *Coach Management on What Should Go to the Board*: This may be the first time an entrepreneur has worked with a board, and they need coaching on when and how to engage with a board. Some issues should be dealt with in a properly convened board meeting, while others should be discussed between the CEO and individual directors outside the board meeting. Boards should expect outside counsel to help the CEO with these judgments.

(Continued)

(Continued)

- *Keep the Cap Table Clean:* Emerging-growth companies have complex cap tables with multiple classes of stock, options for employees, and advisor equity and warrants for debt financing and partner incentives. The average emerging-growth company has a more complex capital structure than most small public companies. Consequently, outside counsel should help maintain good capitalization and other corporate records, including minutes and records of board and stockholder approvals.
- *Be Open to Criticism, Don't Be Defensive, and Request Constructive Feedback:* Lawyers pride themselves on having a high degree of precision. At the same time, business transactions aren't perfect, exigencies often drive sub-optimal results, and outright mistakes sometimes occur. Your outside counsel should be open to hearing those concerns, and your board should have a mechanism to provide this feedback. Generally, everyone learns something from a well-developed feedback loop. And, as with all feedback, provide it early.
- *Never, Ever, Bend the Truth or Be Anything Less Than Transparent:* I rarely have observed an attorney lie, but many are willing to be less than transparent. You should demand absolute transparency with outside counsel. When they live up to this obligation, they shouldn't be criticized by the board or management if there is a disagreement.

Mike Platt, Cooley, Partner

Note

1. Data from Steven Kaplan and Per Stromberg, "Financial Contracting Theory Meets the Real World: Evidence from Venture Capital Contracts," *Review of Economic Studies* 70 (2003): 281–315. An interesting paper on the importance of independent directors is authored by Brian J. Broughman, "Independent Directors and Shared Board Control in Venture Finance" (July 18, 2011). Indiana Legal Studies Research Paper No. 1123840. Available at SSRN: http://ssrn.com/abstract=1123840 or doi:10.2139/ssrn.1123840.

Chapter 5

Board Functions

Early in the life of a company, the board is often small, numbering between three and five people. At this point in the company's development, board business is often presented simultaneously to the entire board. As Paul Berberian (Sphero co-founder, Company Six founder/chair) correctly points out, "In startup boards, there is not much to govern. The board has to support the CEO with their resources, opinions, and their experience—where they see what has worked in other companies and what has not."

The Role of Board Committees

As a company grows, its board of directors and the number of things the board needs to consider also increase. As the level of oversight of the board expands, the board forms specific committees, including audit, compensation, and nominating/governance. Existing board members serve on one or more of these committees. Each committee has a charter describing the responsibilities, including structure, processes, authority, and committee membership, described below.

- **Audit:** Oversees the company's accounting and financial reporting processes and financial audits. The responsibilities include ensuring timely audits, independence of audits, and communicating with the independent auditors about any relationships or services that could affect the auditor's objectivity and independence.

- **Compensation:** Establishes CEO and executive team compensation, oversees equity compensation grant policy, and reviews outside data or hires outside experts to provide opinions as needed on market-based compensation ranges.
- **Nominating/Governance:** Recruits and orients new directors, manages CEO succession planning, and monitors governance processes.

Informal Responsibilities of a Board

The informal responsibilities of a board are just as important as the formal ones. Following are a few to give you a taste of them as we'll go through them in more detail in later chapters.

- **Ensuring Company Survival:** One of the most important tasks of a board member is ensuring the startup stays alive. Startups can run out of cash, face schisms between the founders, or get sued out of existence by patent trolls. Richard Huston (Ohio TechAngels, Founder) points out that the board's main task is to make sure a company never runs out of cash.[1] While no one can guarantee survival, stepping up to help when a company is in distress is a fundamental role of a board member.
- **Establishing Financial Controls:** A board establishes procedures and policies to establish financial controls. These include policies such as two signatories, such as the CEO and CFO, and board approvals for major expenses, often defined as expenses above a certain threshold. From an entrepreneur's perspective, if the board approves an annual operating budget, such controls are easy to handle if any significant deviations occur since the board can approve those instead of the CEO seeking approval for every item. As the company matures, audits of financial statements become the norm, governed by the audit committee. While this process requires considerable time and effort, the board ensures management follows appropriate accounting practices.

- **Developing Reporting Guidelines:** The board should ensure shareholders understand the status of the business. Often a term sheet will include formal reporting requirements. Example language from the term sheet is:

  > *The Company will deliver to such Major Investor (i) annual, quarterly, and monthly financial statements, and other information as determined by the Board; (ii) thirty days prior to the end of each fiscal year, a comprehensive operating budget forecasting the Company's revenues, expenses, and cash position on a month-to-month basis for the upcoming fiscal year; and (iii) promptly following the end of each quarter an up-to-date capitalization table.*

  Regardless of whether formal reporting requirements are defined, actual reporting is the responsibility of the CEO. A good board will encourage a CEO to send these reports out on a regular and predetermined cadence.

- **Conducting CEO Performance Assessment and Resolving Conflicts:** While many companies have an internal review process, this is often overlooked for the CEO. The board can provide the framework for this oversight, which results in a robust annual CEO review. When conflicts between the CEO and co-founders or other management team members arise, the board often plays the role of conflict resolver. For example, an entrepreneur we work with stated: "My co-founder and I were having a lot of conflict on various day-to-day issues. Our VC pulled me aside and said, 'We have one CEO—that's you. You need to put your partner in a box. If you can't do this, you shouldn't be the CEO.' I had to finally learn how to manage my co-founder. We got through it successfully, had a good outcome, and remained friends, but it was tough."

Control Priorities

As explained in *Venture Deals* (Feld and Mendelson, 2019), the two primary characteristics of every investment are economics and control. While economics are often well defined, control is subtler.

The terms regarding control may be decoupled from the actual economics and be buried in the nuances of the financing documents.

A startup can have multiple levels of control. One level is between the CEO and the board. The CEO controls the company's day-to-day business and operating decisions and the allocation of resources to achieve the plan. The CEO sets the annual plan, but the board approves it. The CEO hires and recommends compensation for the next management layer—the board approves it. And usually, the board can fire and replace the CEO.

The founders and non-investor shareholders have various controls based on the number of shares outstanding, specific voting rights, and corporate law. However, this level of control can be elusive after a financing, especially in the context of the *protective provisions* of the investors. The protective provisions can include changing the terms of stock owned by the investors, authorizing the creation of more stock, issuing any stock senior or equal to the investors, buying back any of the common stock, selling the company, changing the certificate of incorporation, or bylaw, changing the size of the board of directors, declaring or paying a dividend, and borrowing money. Investors can also have drag-along rights, which compel other shareholders to vote with them in certain situations. Investors generally have conversion rights, giving them control over converting their preferred stock into common stock.

Separately, board members will have fiduciary duties to all shareholders independent of their status as shareholders. Even if a specific share class, such as the Series A, appoints a director, the director is still responsible to all shareholders. Consequently, the idea of a "Series A Director" who represents the "Series A" is an invalid construct, as this director is simply appointed by the Series A. This dynamic often creates intellectual dissonance for some investor board members, as they struggle in certain situations to determine whether they are playing a board member role or an investor role.

Noam Wasserman (Harvard Business School Professor, author of *The Founder's Dilemmas*, 2012) clearly states the conflict between economics and control. "If you don't figure out which matters more to you, you could end up being neither rich nor king." While some entrepreneurs accomplish being rich and king, they are the exception, not the rule. Wasserman's advice is that if you care more about control, consider not raising any capital. Instead, bootstrap your company. Also, never forget that startups have a high failure rate; many vanish into oblivion, achieving neither fame nor fortune.

Being Rich and Queen (or King)

Occasionally, founders have retained board-level control and economics that last beyond the company's IPO. A few, such as Mark Zuckerberg, have become, in Noam Wasserman's words, both rich and king. To do this, you need to have a large stock position and voting control, which can be achieved even if you don't own more than 50% of the company.

In the case of Facebook, the company created two classes of shares before it went public. At the time of the IPO, Zuckerberg owned 18% of the company. However, he owned Class B shares that had ten votes to every one vote of the Class A shares sold to the public in the IPO. Even though he only owned 28% of the Class B shares, several other founders (who were also Class B shareholders) entered into a voting agreement with Zuckerberg that gave him voting control over 57% of the Class B shares and greater than 50% voting control over the company.

This dual-class approach isn't new. Google went public with a similar structure, and numerous media companies, such as Viacom and News Corp, have dual-class share structures as public companies. In the early 2010s, tech IPOs, including LinkedIn, Groupon, Yelp, and Zynga, used dual-class share structures. This trend has accelerated, with over 30% of recent tech IPOs, including Snap and Dropbox, going public with dual-class share structures.[2]

This dual-class share structure isn't only put in place simply to anoint the CEO Queen or massage a founder/CEO's ego. Instead, it's used to manage the short-term views of many public market investors, who often seek magical results every quarter. This structure can be a defense mechanism in this day of activist shareholders, deterring these investors from exerting inappropriate operating pressure on the company.

Founders can retain control of the board using a dual-class shares structure, but this is an exception, and not the norm, especially in earlier stages of the company's evolution. Some investors are indifferent to it, while others care deeply about linking governance to actual ownership, with the norm being "one share, one vote." VC views continue to evolve, as more VCs either take a stance of being "founder friendly," choose to be indifferent for competitive reasons so they can get into more investments, or just don't pay attention to founder/VC dynamics. When everything goes well, this doesn't matter. But when things don't go well, it can matter a lot.

Establishing dual-class shares before a public offering can be achieved, but these companies need meteoric growth combined with positive CEO and board dynamics. To pull off a dual-class structure, many foundational elements have to align, including the founder/CEO's performance, the growth of the company, and support from the existing board.

Shareholder Rights

The *Shareholder Rights Agreement* describes the rights of shareholders, governed by the *Articles of Incorporation* of the company and the laws of the state in which the company is incorporated. These rights can include:

- **Voting Rights, Including the Right to Elect Directors:** The directors represent the interests of shareholders. Voting rights may be addressed in a separate *Voting Rights Agreement.*
- **Inspection of Corporate Books and Records:** This allows shareholders to review the board's decision-making process and the company's financial records. In some states, such as California, minority shareholders have the right to inspect two different sets of records: (a) record of shareholders, and (b) accounting books, records, and minutes of proceedings. The startup's bylaws cannot modify these rights.

- **Initiating Actions Against Directors for Illegal or Fraudulent Activities:** This right can vary by state. For example, California law[3] states that shareholders can exercise their rights under these conditions:

  - Removal of directors for cause or by court proceedings
  - A director's standard of care
  - Directors and Officers' indemnification
  - The liability of directors and shareholders for unlawful distributions
  - Dissenters' rights
  - Appraisal rights

Economic and Performance Priorities

In contrast to control provisions, which are tightly defined in advance, economic performance is tied to the progress of a startup. As CEO, you and your team are primarily responsible for the company's performance through your daily activities, which impact product, sales, revenue, cash, profits, and ultimately the company's valuation.

If you and your team don't execute effectively, the company's value, and thus the shareholders' financial outcomes, deteriorate. Alternatively, if the company makes excellent progress on milestones but runs out of cash, new or existing investors may propose additional financing at a lower valuation, commonly called a *down round*. When a board approves a financing at a lower valuation than the last round, it negatively impacts all current shareholders.

While the ultimate decision of a board is hiring and firing the CEO, the board also has many responsibilities that affect the company's economics. These include approving the annual budget and operating plan, addressing compensation plans and stock option grants, addressing any financing, debt, or expenses above a certain threshold, and managing and expanding the option pool.

The span of control of the board relative to a CEO differs from company to company. In many startups, the line between the two is blurred. While the CEO is part of the board, clearly delineating the responsibilities, especially around business operations and performance, is critical. See Table 5.1.

Table 5.1 Key responsibilities of the CEO and the board

	CEO	Both CEO and board	Board members
Goals	Sets the overall vision and strategy of the company and communicates it to all stakeholders Recruits, hires, and retains the very best talent for the company Makes sure there's always enough cash in the bank[1]	Ensure alignment, accountability and transparency	Monitor economics, governance, and control Develop policies and procedures to support the CEO and the company
Team	Recruits, hires, evaluates, and fires team members	Develop annual hiring and stock option plan	Hire and fire the CEO Evaluate CEO performance Evaluate board performance
Budget and plan	Develops annual budget and plan for board approval	Review and modify budget and plan	Approve annual budget and plan
Execution	Executes on plan and suggests corrective action	Modify plan based on market conditions	Monitor performance of the company
Operations	Drives product development, sales, and marketing	Ensure policies and processes are established	Confirm and review tax, audit, and regulatory compliance
Financial	Maintains records, accounts, and produces monthly statements	Review performance Make strategic decisions about capital structure	Assist with financing Review audits

[1] From Fred Wilson's spectacular post on "What a CEO Does," AVC, August 30, 2010, http://www.avc.com/a_vc/2010/08/what-a-ceo-does.html (accessed January 7, 2022).

Emotional Priorities: Trust, Judgment, and Transparency

The functional priorities of the board tend to be concrete, well-defined, and legally constructed. In contrast, emotional priorities are qualitative, personality-driven, and fluid.

Trust among board members is essential. You simply won't have an effective board in the absence of trust. While board members have different personalities, divergent goals, and polarizing or conflicting styles, trust is the foundation for the board's success. Trust is hard to earn and easy to lose. If this trust is broken, the board's priority should be to reestablish it.

While trust tends to be binary—it either exists or doesn't—judgment tends to be issue-specific. Board members will have various levels of experience with different problems, impacting individuals' ability to make sound judgments in different situations. Consequently, a board member needs to be self-aware. A board member who recognizes they aren't an expert on a particular issue or explicitly qualifies their confidence in their opinion on a specific matter is a much more valuable board member. Beware board members who know everything and who strongly assert their position on all issues.

Transparency glues together trust and judgment. The board should discuss all issues and opinions openly. Any conflict, especially between board members, should be brought to the entire board to discuss. While there will be one-off discussions between board members or closed sessions that don't include management, ultimately, all issues discussed should be surfaced to all board members. Communicating feedback from the closed session to the CEO is particularly important. This transparency enables a board to function effectively in most circumstances.

Notes

1. From a December 2011 presentation made at Angel Capital Association.
2. Dhruv Aggarwal, Ofer Eldar, Yael V. Hochberg, and Lubomir P. Litov, "The Rise of Dual-Class Stock IPOs." *The CLS Blue Sky Blog*, April 21, 2022, https://clsbluesky.law.columbia.edu/2021/04/21/the-rise-of-dual-class-stock-ipos/ (accessed January 7, 2022).
3. Section 2115 of California General Corporation Law (CGCL). See: http://codes.lp.findlaw.com/cacode/CORP/1/1/d1/21/s2115 (accessed January 7, 2022). This law provides that sections of the CGCL apply to non-California incorporated corporations if (i) more than 50 percent of the corporation's business is conducted in California and (ii) more than 50 percent of their outstanding voting securities are held of record by persons having addresses in California. Section 2115 provides that California law supersedes the law of the jurisdiction of incorporation concerning various matters. We are grateful to Yoichiro "Yokum" Taku's blog www.startupcompanylawyer.com for synthesizing this information.

Section 2

Creating Your Board

Chapter 6

Size and Composition

How large should your board be, and who should be on it? This issue will come up multiple times over the life of your company.

The size of your board is directly related to the stage and complexity of the company. If you are pre-Series A (Startup), then a board of three is plenty. Once you have raised a Series A or Series B (Revenue), a five-person board should be adequate until you raise a later-stage round (Growth) or are starting to think about going public. At that point, your board will often expand to seven or nine people. Recognize that these are general guidelines, not specific rules.

The performance of the board is independent of size. We've been on unruly and ineffective three-person boards and high-octane nine-person boards. Ultimately, the composition and management of the board are more important than the number of people on it.

While it is not a requirement, most boards have an odd number of directors, which helps address the situation where you have a tie vote on an issue. However, during Matt's 20 years as CEO of Return Path, the company had long stretches with four or six directors, and it was never a problem. Matt's view was that if something came down to a tie vote, they had more significant issues.

Your board will have three different types of directors.

- **Management:** Founders, the CEO, or a management team member who works at the company.

- **Investors:** Institutional investors such as VCs. These can also be angel investors or a formal or informal angel group.
- **Independents:** People who are neither company management nor representatives of institutional investors, even if they own some stock options or have made a small angel investment.

Let's discuss each type in depth.

Management

Except for founders, boards should only include one management team member, the CEO. Since boards hire and fire CEOs, having a management team member on the board creates a challenging dynamic. If you are the CEO and Mary reports to you as your VP Revenue, and she's also on the board, then Mary reports to you, but you also effectively report to her. Since a crucial part of the board's role is to hold all management accountable, there's now a circular dynamic between you and Mary.

As a CEO, you have a limited number of board seats to fill. Your board members add outside perspective, strategic advice, and a broad network to the board. In contrast, your management team members are 100% focused on your company, so you're already getting their daily perspective and advice. Adding a second management team member to your board takes away an opportunity to add another outside director who can bring diverse talent and brainpower to your board.

There are several exceptions to this guideline. The first is a co-founder who's still at the company and reporting to you. In the early stages, it's typical to have several founders on the board. As you raise more financing rounds, the board configuration often shifts to a founder seat, and a CEO seat, so if you are a founder/ CEO, you may still have another founder on the board. The other exception occurs later when the founder remains CEO but hires an operating president or COO. Occasionally, this person will get a board seat, especially if they run a large part of the company.

As a company grows, many founder/CEOs realize they don't want another founder on the board, especially if the founder leaves the company because of a difference or conflict with the founder/CEO. An interim solution is for the departing founder to serve as a board observer. However, these observer seats tend to become limited as a company gets closer to going public and ultimately are eliminated in an IPO.

Investors

The director seats held by investors can be challenging to manage because many VCs believe an essential part of their investment is having a board seat. As you get to later rounds, you often find new investors asking for a board seat while the earlier investors insist on keeping their existing board seat. As you negotiate this dynamic, you can often persuade investors to have the right to assign an independent director. Alternatively, many later-stage investors will be willing only to have an observer seat. While this may help, the independent director, in this case, is still linked to the VC firm, and an observer still takes up space in the boardroom.

Seth Levine (Foundry, Partner) wrote a post[1] where he cited a study done by Correlation Ventures showing that there are limits to how many VCs you should have on the board. Spoiler alert: not that many.

> There's value to having VCs on your board. In fact, there's value (or at least a correlation with success) to having multiple VCs on your board. But this value diminishes—and does so rapidly—as you add too many . . . I think it's important to point out here that, at least in my experience, having too many VCs around the table is bad for companies even if those VCs are good, helpful, competent people.

A chart from the Correlation Ventures post[2] shows that companies with more than three investor board members performed worse than those with three or fewer (Figure 6.1).

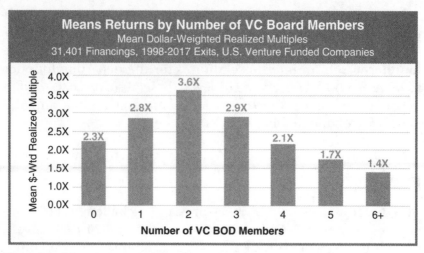

Figure 6.1   Means returns by VC board members.
Source: Correlation Ventures.

Independents

An independent director allows you to bring different sets of experience and perspectives to your board. The independent director provides the perspective of a business operator, functional executive, or customer. Brenda Freeman (founder and CEO of Joyeux Advisors) has been a founder, C-level executive, and independent director on early-stage and global, established companies. She provides seasoned advice about her experience.

You can be incredibly helpful to a board as an independent director, but your effectiveness depends in part on the stage of the company you're working with and your own skills. For example, I have several decades of experience in consumer-facing businesses in both marketing and technology roles, at the C-level for large-scale global corporations, and as a founder/CEO in several startups. I'm also a practicing engineer, so I'm still "in the game" and current in the areas of business, technology, and marketing. When I'm serving on the board of an early-stage company, I'm providing advice based on my functional expertise, but the role requires me to stay at about 10,000 feet. Even though I can provide operational advice, doing so is crossing a line, and the true role of a board director is governance and holding the CEO accountable, not being a consultant to them.

On the other hand, when I'm on the board of an established, legacy company, I'm typically the youngest person on the board. In this situation, the board and company have a standing culture. With an established company, many of the board seats have been filled with the same people for a long time, so there's consistency in how things are done. There are established relationships, and the issues are well-defined. I'm often the only woman or the only person of color on the board, so my true value is to add my perspective—not to "tell them what to do." I've found that asking very good questions—even simple questions—can be a powerful way to add value since it forces people to think carefully about their assumptions and ways of doing things. In large-scale companies one of the best things you can do as an independent director is develop strong relationships with the other members because that leads to credibility and trust, and those are the currency of making an impact.

Brenda Freeman, Joyeux Advisors, founder and CEO

Matt's Rule of 1s

Unless you are focused on controlling the board, try to create a balanced board. Building a balanced board can be challenging since you are simultaneously trying to get the right balance of the three types of directors while also getting a mix of skills and experience relative to your stage as a company.

Over the years, Matt came up with a simple approach, which he called the "Rule of 1s," that allows you to be intentional about building and managing your board.

Build your board purposefully and with independence from Day 1.

Have 1 member of the management team on your board (the CEO).

For every 1 investor director, appoint 1 independent director.

While you don't need to follow Matt's Rule of 1s, and might not be able to if you have a co-founder on your board, it's a great heuristic to manage the development of your board, especially in the later stages of your company when independent directors become even more critical.

Notes

1. Seth Levine, "You May Have Too Many VCs on Your Board," *VC Adventure*, March 13, 2018. https://www.sethlevine.com/archives/2018/03/you-may-have-too-many-vcs-on-your-board.html (accessed January 7, 2022).
2. David Coats, "Too Many VC Cooks in the Kitchen?," *Medium*, March 13, 2018. https://medium.com/correlation-ventures/too-many-vc-cooks-in-the-kitchen-65439f422b8 (accessed January 7, 2022).

Chapter 7

VCs and Boards

Not all VC board members understand their unique role. We've been involved with boards where VCs believe that their job is to provide "adult supervision" to entrepreneurs. We find this language to be pejorative and insulting to entrepreneurs. Some VCs feel the need to manage the CEO and the entrepreneurs. Others can't help but get involved in minutia, try to solve emerging problems, and stir up conflict. This type of VC board member gets in the way, confuses the management team, and, in the worst case, damages the startup.

If you're looking for capital from VCs for your startup, it'll come with strings attached, including at least one VC board member. Be prepared to deal with various mindsets and personalities, as VCs aren't a singular archetype. As Brad wrote on his blog:

> Think about D&D [Dungeons and Dragons], or Magic the Gathering, or any other game like that. The VCs are individual characters in D&D. Each character has a different set of skills, weapons, money, and experience points and over time develops more. A firm is a combination of different characters—at Foundry, you might have a mage and a barbarian—and the combination is what you have to pay attention to.[1]

The challenge of raising the first round of capital is well documented. This challenge continues to be true for the second, third, and next rounds of capital for many companies. Despite the long odds, many companies need capital. Raising financing, especially the first round, is a significant achievement—it's validation of you, your team, or your product.

Once you raise the first round of capital, a new set of challenges arises. Investors are looking for substantial financial returns. They want you to make demonstrable progress and achieve certain milestones. They may also be looking for new rounds of financing at higher prices or even quick exits—both of which increase the value of their investment. While some investors may be patient, taking a decade or longer view to helping build the company, others are more anxious to see quick progress. Often, these investors view the company as partly their own, which is true now that they are investors. Some of these investors are happy to support the entrepreneur. Others have their own view of what the entrepreneur should be doing.

When a term sheet is on the horizon, many founders are ecstatic that the process of raising financing is almost over. At this point, some founders ignore the type of board members that come with the money. Smart founders understand that building a great company is all about the people, and the board members are just as important as the early employees. "If I was prepping my younger brother on a startup journey, I would tell him to raise money only from those investors who can strategically add value and emotionally connect with you to help you be better," says Jason Mendelson (Foundry, Partner Emeritus). Choose your VCs wisely.

Once you've raised money, the VC will ensure their investment has some protection due to control provisions in the financing documents. The VC will also have a governance role if they take a board seat. While founders and investors often fret over control issues, Fred Wilson (Union Square Ventures, Partner) points out, "Boards should not be controlled by the founder, the CEO, or the largest shareholder. For a board to do its job, it must represent all stakeholders' interests, not just one stakeholder's interest."[2]

VCs typically conduct a significant amount of due diligence on the founders, the CEO, and the management team before investing in a company. Entrepreneurs should do the same with prospective investors and board members. In assessing fit, entrepreneurs should look at individual attributes while also considering group dynamics. The composition of the board and the interplay between different board members are the first steps in assessing prospective board members.

A great board member who's part of a less-than-stellar VC firm is like a great singer in a lousy band where neither benefits from the other, undermining what can be good about each of them. The opposite is also true—having a less-than-stellar board member from a great VC firm won't be helpful. As you evaluate VCs, pay attention to the following three areas as you explore their firm.

- **Capital:** Can the VC firm's current fund invest across multiple rounds of your company? If it's not clear, ask the VC you are dealing with to understand how their firm approaches future financings, how they reserve capital for follow-on financings, and whether they require a new investor to lead subsequent rounds. Ask how much capital they have available in their fund for future investments. If VCs are tight regarding capital, that can constrain your ability to grow quickly and lead to desperate measures by VCs who focus only on their short-term returns and ignore all other shareholders.
- **Firm Stability and Individual Tenure:** How long have the partners in the firm worked together? Is the partner you are talking to new to the firm? Has there been recent turnover or changes in the partners at the firm? Instead of relying on articles in the tech press, ask other entrepreneurs for their perception of the firm. While some of the best VCs are relatively new to the business or junior in their firms, having your entire board filled with VCs just learning the business can be a problem, especially in difficult or complex situations. If you find yourself working with a junior partner at a firm, you should insist on having a personal relationship with one of the senior partners and touch base with them a few times a year. At Return Path, Matt's board member from Flatiron Partners left the firm early on. Matt was proactive about his relationship with Fred Wilson, resulting in Fred quickly joining and integrating into the board.
- **Strong Portfolio with Demonstrated Exits:** A VC firm's future depends on its ability to generate returns. If it doesn't have a strong portfolio or meaningful exits, it may not be on solid ground. If a VC firm is struggling, the partners may

focus on issues separate or divergent from yours, such as the survival of their firm, interpersonal conflicts between partners, or short-term exits in their portfolio.

A combination of the VC firm's financial strength, stability, stature, and individual attributes of the partners impacts your startup. Many CEOs get caught up in the flamboyance of a resume or the historical reputation of a particular VC or the firm. Jaclyn Hester, a partner at Foundry, points out the mistake entrepreneurs make when they look for the famous, superstar board member:

> *You should find the most prestigious and pedigreed board member you can find. But there's so much more to what makes a great board member for you and your company. Some questions to consider include: Do I like and trust this individual? How will this person show up in the boardroom? Does this person bring a relevant perspective? Will this person be responsive, available, and supportive? Will this person tell me the truth?*

If you want a more thorough explanation of the dynamics within a VC firm, *Venture Deals* covers it in the chapter entitled "How Venture Capital Firms Work" (Feld and Mendelson, 2019).

Notes

1. Brad Feld, "VCs Are Like D&D Characters," Feld Thoughts, August 2, 2012. https://feld.com/archives/2012/08/vcs-are-like-dd-characters.html (accessed January 7, 2022).
2. Fred Wilson, "The Board of Directors' Role and Responsibilities," https://avc.com/2012/03/the-board-of-directors-role-and-responsibilities/, (n. 3).

Chapter 8

Board Evolution

The size and composition of your board form the foundation that helps your company scale—otherwise, it's just a collection of people. Considering board dynamics over time is essential since the board you start with isn't necessarily the one that will grow with you. It's important to think through the skills and experiences of board members since what you need as a startup in a board member could be a hindrance, distraction, or obstacle as you scale.

While a person with strong finance, audit, regulatory, and cost-control expertise would be a suitable board member for a growth company preparing for an IPO, they're less effective for a startup of three people that's pre-product and pre-revenue.

In the early stages of a company, the founders should lead the board formation process. As a company evolves, responsibility for the configuration and evolution of the board shifts to the CEO and the largest investors. As the company continues to grow and board interactions become more formalized, the board typically forms a *nominating/governance committee* consisting of several board members, including the CEO and/or a founder. In all of these cases, board members should actively contribute to defining the board's composition.

Startup Stages

In Chapter 6, we discussed the three stages of growth that impact your board: *Startup, Revenue,* and *Growth.* Table 8.1 summarizes

Table 8.1   The role of board members at different stages of a company

Role of Board Member/ Company Needs	Startup Working/ Active	Revenue Shaping/ Nurturing	Growth Governing/ Monitoring
Strategy	High	High	High
Recruiting	High	High	High
Customer discovery and market development	High	Moderate	Low
Product development	High	Moderate	Low
Sales and marketing	High	High	Medium
Finance and operational controls	Moderate	Moderate	High
Human Resources	Low	Moderate	High

the role of board members at each stage. However, it's difficult to figure out how to evolve your board across stages or even recognize when transitioning between stages.

When a company participates in multiple financings, each round often comes with a new lead investor who usually insists on a board seat. If you don't manage your board configuration deliberately, it's easy to end up with a five- or seven-person board dominated by investors. Even if you include independent director seats in financing agreements, these often go unfilled until the founders and CEO prioritize building the board.

The best thing you can do is establish multiple independent board seats early on before you raise much money, and then limit the number of investor seats as the board grows, per Matt's Rule of 1s in Chapter 6.

It's unlikely that an investor will insist on removing a qualified independent director. It's also unlikely that investors will be excited about sitting on a nine-person board early in a company's life since there isn't enough complexity for them to make a significant contribution. By holding firm on the number of independents and the total size of the board, you'll force the difficult conversation about board configuration, specifically which investors get board seats and which ones become board observers. This will happen with all of your investor board members each time you raise a new round of financing.

While you may get pushback from new investors on limiting the number of investor board members, forcing the conversation will result in more deliberate board construction. If you prioritize having a diverse board, it'll reinforce a strategy of having a significant number of non-investor independent directors on the board. However, there are two tactics you can use to address investor angst around board configuration.

Limiting the Number of Investor Board Members

By changing the mix of covenants in your corporate governance documents, you'll give groups of shareholders specific voting rights or blocks so that not all critical decisions are approved only by a board vote. As a result, even if investors don't have a board seat or board vote, they'll still have a voice in matters they care about influencing. This is often covered comprehensively in the protective provisions of the term sheet for a financing, so it's a useful way to align the financing documents, board voting responsibility, and shareholder voting responsibility. However, be careful not to add too many restrictive covenants. Also, be thoughtful about voting thresholds so that you don't inadvertently give an individual shareholder or a class of shareholders a block on a particular item. This issue is covered extensively in *Venture Deals* (Feld and Mendelson, 2019).

Another tactic is to have an investor director designate a non-investor to hold their board seat. While you should expect such a designee to align with the interests of the investor who controls their appointment, this person will have the fiduciary duty of all directors to put the company's interests first. Appointing non-investors to the board enables collaboration with the investor to add more diversity to the board.

Many VC firms have a group of experienced operators they recruit to take board seats. Others, especially firms with limited gender or racial diversity, have active programs to get women and people of color onto boards or use services like Him for Her, BoardList, or Bolster to find qualified board members from diverse backgrounds. Over the past few years, this trend has accelerated, so it's no longer a rare exception for an investor to be willing to put a non-investor operator in a board seat designated to the VC.

Recognize that some VCs either have an ego attachment to or functional reasons for a board seat. How will it look to their fellow GPs if they get kicked off a board? Did the VC's partners expect them to stay on the board when the firm approved the initial investment? Do the LPs of the firm expect that the GPs are going to maintain their board seats? Understanding the expectations of board members and resetting them, or at least discussing them, is an integral part of board evolution.

Managing Independent Seats

While investor director seats link to financings, independent director seats do not. Consequently, it is important to consider and implement term lengths for independent board members.

Early on, think of an independent director the same way you'd think about a senior executive. While you'll be excited the day the person says yes to joining your board, you won't know if they are a good fit until you've had some run time with them.

We've been on boards with independent directors for a decade where they've been excellent board members every step of the way. We've also been on boards with independent directors who were brilliant, but only for the first few meetings. By meeting four, they simply repeated the same few statements or pieces of advice. Or, they were inconsistent about showing up and were hard to nail down for opinions or decisions and just parroted back what the CEO seemed to want to do.

Building a board is the same as building your management team. Even if they appear awesome on day one, some people simply won't work out over the longer term. Others will scale out, or a life priority will change that limits their ability or interest in engaging as a board member. Defining an exact length for the board term upfront eliminates the awkwardness of firing an ineffective board member. If the board member is performing well, simply extend the term. If not, graciously thank the board member for their service and replace them with a new independent director when their term ends.

In Matt's new company, Bolster, independent directors get either a one- or two-year term, with a commensurate option grant that vests over the period. If the director is effective, they stay on for another one- or two-year term and get an additional option grant. This short-term length creates a forcing function for all parties to determine whether the relationship is working as the company grows and changes.

Chapter 9

What to Look for in a Director

Entrepreneurs put tremendous energy into recruiting a phenomenal VP of Engineering, hiring the best developers, and building an amazing sales organization. But when attracting board members, many entrepreneurs are casual, or even passive, about recruiting great board members—or don't do it at all.

But what makes a good director? Just like it is difficult to find your way from point A to point B for the first time without directions, a map, or a GPS, it's similarly difficult to find a good board member without putting together a job specification or requirements document to guide the process. While hiring an independent board member is no different than hiring a senior executive, we often see CEOs running board searches with nothing more than "I want a more experienced CEO in our industry" as a job description.

The job spec for a board member differs from that of an executive because you are looking for more than just functional competencies (e.g., "someone who knows how to be a board member"). You are looking for the right combination of experience, soft skills, and governance philosophy to meet your company's needs.

General Skills

The best board members are prepared, keep their commitments, and show up to all meetings. They're punctual, don't leave early, and are fully present during meetings.

The board member develops relationships independent of the CEO throughout the organization, including other board members, management team members, project leaders, and other key employees. Some CEOs are uncomfortable with board members developing these relationships because of a loss of control. Rather than avoiding addressing this, a good CEO will work with the board to define the rules of engagement around this type of communication.

Great board members speak their minds, even if a topic is difficult, uncomfortable, or controversial. The best board members are honest, candid, and willing to talk publicly about whatever they are thinking. Matt once had a board member tell him and his entire management team that he needed to be better at firing executives quickly. While this was extreme, it was also refreshing in the moment.

Board members should be strategically engaged but operationally distant. It's nearly impossible for a board member, no matter how experienced or talented, to parachute into a board meeting and be helpful with a tactical, operational decision. The best board members know that there are nuances, specifics, and complexities to every business, market, and ecosystem, so they'll take a backseat on providing operational advice. Instead, they'll be strategically engaged in the fundamental dynamics of your business, team, markets, growth opportunities, and challenges.

Fit with Your Existing Board

As with any functioning team, alignment between cultural norms and values is essential to effective working relationships. For a new director, will their style, cultural norms, and values work with your existing board? Does the director need to be particularly financially fluent? Are they comfortable challenging others, the status quo, or widely held assumptions? Are you looking for someone who will roll up their sleeves and do hands-on operational work with management, or do you want someone with name recognition? Does the person have a reputation for engaging in challenging experiences, or are they someone who is around when things are going great but vanishes when times get tough?

Executive teams can recruit, hire, and then fire a high-performing executive because the alignment isn't there or the new team member struggles to operate effectively and have an impact. Boards are no different.

What Does Your Company Need?

When doing a board search, use the metaphor of a team to determine what kind of skills you need. What kind of team is your board, what type of team do you want or need it to be? As a result, what type of player are you trying to recruit? Consider different types of teams. The Three Tenors can't go out and find the best possible singer to replace a retiring star. They must find a tenor! Surgical teams consist of nurses, surgeons, and anesthesiologists. Each is important but hardly interchangeable. Sports teams are full of athletes. Again, they're not all interchangeable in (American) Football or Baseball, but they get a lot closer to interchangeable in Football (Soccer) or Basketball.

Consider your strengths and weaknesses along with those of your company. Define the gaps you and your team have and the experience you need to fill the gaps. Consider what you need now, not in some theoretical future. Do you need someone who can open doors in a critical vertical market? Help with key buyers, customers, or influencers? Have experience in complex sales processes? If you are an engineering-heavy team lacking go-to-market experience, consider a director with a strong sales and marketing background. If you're a visionary CEO, explore directors with deep operational experience.

Understand and prioritize the experiences and attributes you desire. You're unlikely to find everything you want in a single person, so rank the relative importance and the tradeoffs, focusing on finding a director who will have a near-term impact.

Experiences

While the general skills described above will apply to all board members, specific experiences and skills will vary widely. Following are some categories to consider:

- **Prior Board or Board-Equivalent Experience:** While you might have prior board experience as the primary criterion for a new board member, this limits your opportunities to add diverse candidates to the board since many who are board-ready won't have previously served on a board. Rather than focus only on prior board experience, consider board-readiness attributes, such as regular interaction with a corporate board, experience in an advisory role, or experience serving on a community or nonprofit board. These broader experiences open up the possibility of identifying potential board members who have different experiences and are more likely to add diversity to the board. However, make sure that your board has at least one director with experience serving on a corporate board. If you are first-time founders on the board who have never seen the inside of a boardroom and haven't yet added a VC to the mix, you'll want an independent director who knows how boards operate.

- **Entrepreneurial Experience:** Experience as a founder, CEO, or executive in an entrepreneurial company is desirable, especially for early-stage company board members. There are endless arguments about whether VCs who were once entrepreneurs are better than VCs who were never entrepreneurs. The same debate applies to board members. However, VCs who have never been entrepreneurs can have extraordinary amounts of entrepreneurial experience based on the companies they've invested in. People with limited entrepreneurial experience can still be desirable, as Joanna Rees (CEO of West Ventures) states. "I've been on numerous venture-backed and public company boards but when I joined my first corporate board I had no experience except a nonprofit and my kids' school boards. There's value in that because I had to learn to have my voice heard at the table; I had to figure out how to find common ground. Entrepreneurial experience is a nice-to-have but being able to clearly communicate your perspective and work with people effectively is a must-have for board members."

- **Stage Transition Experience:** Some companies find it particularly challenging to move from one stage of growth to another. For a B2B SaaS company, the transition from startup to revenue can be challenging. For a Direct-to-Consumer (DTC) company, an entrepreneurial friend of Matt's says, "Getting to $100 million in sales for a DTC business is not that hard. Getting beyond that can be next to impossible if you don't have a broad enough vision of how your product and future products can fit into the retail landscape." It's powerful for a director to have specific experience navigating the ins and outs of a stage transition.
- **Domain Expertise:** It's helpful for the director to have a strong network and connections within your industry or market. "When building a board, you should focus on a mix of experience, looking beyond just industry knowledge. Based on your strategy for the next five years, select members with domain expertise for the opportunities and challenges ahead of you. That might look like a mix of marketing and international growth, or even specific to scaling operations or planned fundraising. This is especially important if you are facing opportunities that you, as a founder/CEO, don't have experience in," says Linda Findley (President and CEO, Blue Apron).
- **Customer-Type Experience:** Another dimension to consider is the type of customer your company sells to—large enterprises, mid-market, SMB, or individual consumer. The type of sale, whether direct or through resellers, and the type of sales and product motion, such as PLG (product-led growth), are also relevant.
- **Functional Experience:** Adding a board member with specific functional experience where your team lacks depth and could use more is helpful. As companies mature and start thinking about an IPO, they often look to add an independent director with finance and accounting experience to chair the board's Audit Committee. But early-stage companies can also benefit from focusing on functional experience in board

recruiting. Some executive teams and boards are long on product and tech and need sales, marketing, business development, or customer success experience. Others are more focused on marketing and sales and need a counterweight on the board who is a product or technology expert.

Another way to think of the experience a board member has is through their specific skills on several dimensions. Table 9.1 breaks down the specific skills of great, bad, and terrible potential board members.

Table 9.1   Different skills of a board member

Skills	Great	Beware	Avoid
Entrepreneurial	Has started several companies and hired great teams Understands customer discovery and validation	Worked with larger companies Has a consulting background that isn't an obvious fit	Has fantasized about startups but has never been remotely involved with one Unable to prioritize or deal with ambiguity
Domain expertise	Has hands-on experience in building products in similar markets	Market awareness via secondary sources Lacks depth, but may have potential	Knows the obvious Asks random and annoying questions like "What's your cloud strategy?"
Business development skills	Has developed a value proposition, a sales pitch for a new product in an emerging market, identified early adopters, closed orders, and generated revenue	Has sold products in established and mature markets Met quotas Doesn't necessarily have the creativity or persistence to sell new products	Looks forward to having coffee, accumulating frequent flyer miles, and having fancy lunches
Financial expertise	Has raised multiple rounds of capital leading to a successful exit Generated returns for all stakeholders	Understands financials but hasn't raised capital, dealt with VCs, sold a company, or taken one public	Thinks a balance sheet is used while doing the downward-facing-dog yoga pose
Legal expertise	Understands contracts, legal and regulatory guidelines around finance, taxation, and employment	Demonstrates baseline business judgment acumen Has never been sued	Doesn't realize what could land you in jail Naïve

Attributes

While the experiences of a board member may vary based on the needs of the company and the existing board, there are several key attributes of a great board member:

- **Integrity:** As Warren Buffett says, "Somebody once said that in looking for people to hire, you look for three qualities: integrity, intelligence, and energy. And if they don't have the first, the other two will kill you. If you hire somebody without the first, you really want them to be dumb and lazy." If someone lacks integrity, that's a deal-breaker.
- **Bold Mindset:** The trajectory of a high-growth company is usually a rollercoaster ride without the barf bags. A board member should be comfortable with ambiguity, rapidly changing situations, unexpected crises, and imperfect information. They should have a bias for action and process new information quickly. Brutal honesty, especially calling out weaknesses and problems when they arise, is a treasure while delivering feedback calmly and constructively.
- **Emotional Balance:** A board works best if the board members stay focused. There will be times of levity and joking around, along with periods when individuals share personal challenges. Informal interactions make the board enjoyable and help develop personal relationships. But, ultimately, good board members stay on task during meetings, don't serve up banal platitudes, blather on like a perpetual Pollyanna, or endlessly ask questions.

Governance Philosophy

Philosophical alignment across the board is critically important. Some board members believe in Reed Hastings' famous line that "a board's only role is to hire/fire/compensate the CEO." Others believe that a board's role is to engage deeply with a company's strategy, management team, and operations.

Some directors subscribe to the view that their responsibility is only to maximize shareholder value, while others have a broader perspective that the responsibility of a director is to maximize the value of all stakeholders, including employees, customers, vendors, the community, and society at large.

There's not a right or wrong answer to these questions. Instead, be aware of your directors' philosophy on these topics and whether you want your board to align on any particular one or intentionally diverge to foster robust debate on relevant issues.

Chapter 10

Recruiting and Interviewing Board Members

Once you know what you're looking for in the ideal new board member, you can start the task of recruiting and interviewing candidates. This process is time-consuming, and there aren't any shortcuts or workarounds. You can't delegate this to your head of HR or your executive recruiter, although you can rely on them to help you with the process. However, it's worth every minute you invest, given the leverage a great board provides.

Sourcing

While you often start with people you know, including other entrepreneurs, your investors, attorneys, or recruiters, you shouldn't stop there. Working with organizations that run independent director searches for private companies, especially those that help hire diverse directors, such as Him for Her, BoardList, Bolster, and Above Board, are quick and cost-effective.

Begin by creating a job description that describes the attributes you desire. At the same time, do some brainstorming with your board about who would be your ideal candidate and make a list of actual names. This top-down/bottom-up process is powerful as it'll help you tune the job description while surfacing potential candidates you might not have considered.

For many of us, our own biases of what we perceive "a strong resume" looks like may be getting in the way. Here are a few tips to avoid those biases and find diverse candidates.

- *No experience at a "name brand" tech company.* You assume they are not smart enough to get hired by a brand-name company, but it could mean that they wanted to develop more skills in a smaller company. Look for skills, not titles and company names.
- *No past board experience.* You assume they aren't strategic or experienced enough to add value in the boardroom, but it could mean they haven't had the opportunity. Look for experience on other types of boards, such as nonprofits, homeowners associations, or PTAs.
- *Gaps in resume.* You assume their skills are outdated, but it could mean they purposely took a break from work for a personal or professional reason. Look for how they frame the skills they gained during that time.
- *No C-level experience.* You assume they don't have the strategic experience as an operator to work on your board, but it could mean that titles don't mean as much as function. Look for other executive-level skills like visionary or managing multiple businesses.
- *University attended.* You assume a top-tier university indicates intelligence, but it could mean the candidate got accepted because of privilege or connections. Look for people with a growth mindset in education or technical training.

It's important to run "bias checks" on the candidate review process because things aren't always as they might appear.

Bethany Crystal and Cathy Hawley, Bolster Networks

Once you have your ideal director profile and a list of ideal candidates, start making calls or asking for introductions. Building a board is one of a CEO's powerful calling cards. You can get interesting meetings with stretch candidates you think could be out of your reach but could be helpful to your company.

Without being disingenuous, simply say, "I'm the CEO of Awesome Company and would like to talk to you about a potential board seat with my company" as an entrée. Over the years, Matt has met some of the most important, senior, brand-name people in his industry with this candid approach. You never know what opportunities you'll uncover along the way. Even if the person you contact isn't interested, they'll often recommend others who might be or suggest potential business opportunities between their company and yours.

Lesa Mitchell (Techstars, General Manager) amplifies these points:

> We ask entrepreneurs to identify the three people who could change the trajectory of their company due to their experience, skills, and networks. If you can find people that bring global knowledge and experience in a related area that will add substantial value to your company, seek them out and sell them on the idea of being an advisor or a board member. If those people are all in your neighborhood, you aren't thinking big enough. There's a tendency to fill these valuable board seats with individuals who have never scaled a company. I learned a lesson over the years that some mentors and advisors can give you harmful advice. You have to be picky! Talk to other entrepreneurs who have scaled companies, talk to C-level executives who have access to the networks and experience you need. This is your company, and the decisions regarding advisors or board members are all on you. Make it count.
>
> Lesa Mitchell, Techstars, General Manager

The Interview Process

Following is Matt's interview framework to get the amazing people to join his boards at Return Path, Bolster, and other boards he's chaired:

- **Take the Process Seriously:** Devote as much focus to building your board as to building your executive team, both in thinking through the overall composition and the effort you put in. It's easy to get side-tracked and focus on one person rather than think of a board that evolves and changes over time. Remember that the board's value is much more than one person, and your needs will change over time.
- **Interview Many People:** Have thoughtful, candid, and extensive conversations with each potential board member. They aren't applying for a job, so don't treat them like a job applicant. If you can, have multiple in-person (or via video) meetings, including conversations where you turn the tables and

let the potential board member interview you. Once you've whittled down your list to a few candidates, introduce them to your existing board members and let them have their conversations. Finally, have at least one, and if possible several, members of your leadership team talk to the candidates. As with any interview process, systematically collect data from each person who talks to the candidate and have a conversation with the candidate where you listen to them to get feedback on their views of each person they talk to.

- **Check References:** While checking references is tedious and sometimes disruptive for high-powered people, it's an important part of the process. Learn more about your potential board members from multiple sources and different contexts. If they've served on other boards, speak to CEOs, VCs, or independent directors with whom they've worked. If you're doing due diligence on a first-time director candidate, find a CEO for whom they've worked or advised or a board member who knew them from a previous company. Ascertain whether your prospective board member has enough time for you and your company. Do they have the experiences and attributes you thought they had? Will they fit culturally with the rest of your board?

  Examples of questions that go deeper than typical reference checks include:
  - Describe a few tangible examples of how this board member can help a startup.
  - How did this board member respond to a challenging situation, such as running out of cash or navigating a down round?
  - What are some shortcomings of this person?
  - Who else should be serving on the board with this candidate to fill in their gaps or weaknesses?

Ask open-ended questions. Give the reference a chance to talk and, when you hear something interesting, nudge them along for more information. Don't view this as a check-the-box exercise. You are looking for detailed information about the person you consider joining a critical part of your team.

- **Have Finalists Audition by Attending a Board Meeting:** Don't just invite them to show up. Give them some extra time to read materials in advance and spend time answering any questions they have before the meeting. Having them attend and engage at the meeting is an excellent way to see how they'll fit into your board, contribute, and add perspective. Ideally, you'll set up the discussion with the full board, so the prospective board member feels comfortable engaging in the meeting rather than just sitting and observing. It's a warning sign if the candidate is deferential, afraid of saying something provocative or disagreeing with other opinions. Matt had a candidate, who was considered a sure thing, attend a board meeting and showed up this way. While disappointing, Matt was glad he and his board had seen the candidate in action before offering an option grant and a multi-year term.

- **Sell as Much as You Interview:** As with any executive recruiting process, you want to be selling the role and the company to the candidate at every step. Be enthusiastic about the company, the board you're trying to create, and your long-term vision. But, be honest about yourself and your company, especially around where help is needed. There should be no secrets on a board, and surprises will always set you back, tarnish your credibility, and make it more difficult to create a vibrant board. You want the candidate to know that you need help with product-market fit, have a difficult cap table, or struggle with a co-founder. You want them to understand your weaknesses as a CEO, that you need to work on your written communication skills, or that you feel out of your depth at this stage and are looking for help leveling up. Recognize that your authenticity around these issues is another form of selling, and by exposing your weaknesses, you also reinforce your strengths.

- **Don't Fear Rejecting Potential Board Members:** Even if you like them or consider them to be a business hero or mentor, you should feel comfortable rejecting them if you don't feel awesome about them through this process. Your board is your inner circle. You'll confide in them, and their opinions and insights will impact your entire company.

They'll tell you when you're wrong, when you've got a boneheaded idea, and when you need to develop particular skills.

- **Give the Most Gracious Rejection of Your Career to Runners-up:** When you tell a potential board candidate that you aren't moving forward with them, do it in the most gracious and over-the-top way you can since they are influencers, senior people, thought leaders, and heavy hitters. You want them to feel good about your interaction and speak well about you and your company to others. Ideally, they'd be willing to open doors for you, be an ally, and be part of your network. Also, you may want to revisit them as an advisor or a potential director as your needs change over time. Matt's approach is that everyone he interviews for a board seat gets a handwritten thank-you note. Finalists who don't get selected but go through multiple interviews get a bottle of wine, a handwritten note, and occasionally a modest advisor option grant. Your formula could be different, but you want them to appreciate you and understand that you don't feel like it's a good fit right now.

Interviewing VCs Before They Join Your Board

You may think this advice only applies to independent directors, but we strongly urge CEOs to go through the same process for vetting a future venture investor who will have a board seat. This is more important, as removing a poor-performing VC director from your board is harder. The best VCs will have nothing to hide and appreciate and understand your process since they also do extensive reference checking. Some will give you a list of all the CEOs they've ever worked with or will simply offer to make any introductions you want, including to CEOs they've backed, whom they've fired, or whose companies have failed. If a VC is hesitant to do this, it's a red flag.

Chapter 11

Compensation

Assuming you've managed to attract some awesome board members, how do they get paid? The answer is: it depends.

VCs and Management

You should never pay a VC who sits on your board representing an investment. Their firms are paying the VC to make investments and sit on boards. This is their job. Most VCs have provisions in their agreements with their limited partners (LPs) that either expressly forbid payment or require the VC to remit any compensation they make as a board member back to their funds or as an offset to management fees.

Occasionally, a VC will ask for additional compensation for sitting on your board, usually in the form of a stock option grant. If this is early in the life of your company, it should raise a red flag about that particular VC. If there was a specific agreement negotiated at the time of the investment, that's fine, but a request after the fact is inappropriate. The one exception is after a company has gone public, where some VCs will request a standard board options grant to continue serving on a public company board.

While there should be no board compensation for investor directors, we've seen situations where private equity (PE) firms come into deals, either as minority shareholders or control investors, and want director compensation. Beware of this. If they are coming into an existing syndicate as a minority shareholder and asking for a director fee, tell them no, that isn't your model.

If they buy a controlling interest in the company, it's their decision, not yours, but try to find this out ahead of time. It's a red flag that your new owner, who's already making a lot of money on management fees from their LPs, feels compelled to take more money out of your operating budget for doing their job.

Members of management or founders who sit on the board shouldn't be compensated separately for their board service.

You should reimburse all board members for reasonable expenses incurred on your company's behalf, either for attending board meetings or specific work approved in advance. However, make sure that you have a direct conversation early on about what the definition of "reasonable" is. For some, reasonable means Motel 6, and for others, it means the Four Seasons. For some, it means flying coach. For others, it means buying a first-class ticket. Either way, don't let yourself be surprised after the fact.

Independent Directors

You should compensate independent directors for their board service. Until your company is profitable, you should never use cash as board member compensation. Board members should be willing to take stock, almost always in the form of stock options, and play for the upside. A board member who feels your cash is better off with them rather than investing in hiring another engineer or salesperson is probably not focused on the right things.

A good rule of thumb for an independent director is a stock option grant of the company's stock in the range of 0.25% to 1% of the company that vests from two to four years. The absolute amount varies, and grants are larger earlier in the company's life. One way to size the grant is to think of it as 25% to 50% of what you'd give to a VP-level hire at any point in time.

Bolster ran a Board Benchmark study of stock option grant size for directors of hundreds of private, venture-backed companies in 2020 and 2021. While the data has a wide range to it, the above rules of thumb were reasonably consistent with the survey results, which is broken up into company size/stage as noted by most recent financing (Table 11.1).

Table 11.1 Director option grant size by financing round

Stage	Seed/A	Series B	Series C	Series D
Range: BPS/year	10–30	12–25	5–12	4–10
Average BPS/year	17	15	9	7

BPS, or basis points, is a financial metric where 100 BPS = 1% of the company. To get a full option grant, take the number of BPS/year and multiply it by the number of years the option grant vests.

Following is another way to calculate the amounts from a post from Fred Wilson:[1]

For compensation, I like to use an annual amount of $100,000. That is substantially less than public company directors make (which is more like $200,000 per year), but being a public company director is more time-consuming and exposes a director to more liability. So I feel like $100,000 a year is reasonable compensation for a private company director. The spread between private company board compensation and public company board compensation narrows as a company gets closer to being public.

Private company directors are usually compensated in stock, not cash. I like to use the following approach for stock-based compensation:

For companies valued below $40mm enterprise value, pay an independent director 0.25% of the Company per year served on the Board.

For companies valued above $40mm of enterprise value, pay an independent director a percentage of the Company per year served equal to ($100k/enterprise valuation). For example, if your Company is worth $100mm, then you would pay 0.1% per year served ($100k/$100mm).

It is typical to make a "front-loaded" grant of four years of value and vest it over four years. So in this second example, where the Company is worth $100mm, the independent director would be granted an option for 0.4% of the Company, worth $400k, and vest that over four years.

However, for very early stage companies where the annual grants are quite large (0.25% per year), it is more common to make those grants annually so that the dilution from these grants comes down as the Company's value increases. That said, front-loaded four-year grants are made for directors of early-stage companies as well.

Fred Wilson, Union Square Ventures, Partner

Following are several additional elements of a compensation package for an independent board member.

- **Equity Instrument:** The standard equity instrument for directors is Non-Qualified Stock Options priced at fair market value. If your company gives Restricted Stock or Restricted Stock Units, you can offer those instead. If possible, try to use an instrument that optimizes tax treatment.
- **Vesting Period:** We're proponents of doing smaller, shorter vest option grants, at least for early-stage companies whose needs are dynamic. We suggest grants of one to two years, which is below the standard practice of a four-year vesting term. You can always renew a director's term and give a new grant down the road. If you are at a later stage and are confident you'll want a director for a more extended period, use the standard four-year vesting model.
- **Acceleration Provisions:** For directors, we suggest giving them 100% vesting on an acquisition, legally called a "change of control." While this can occasionally lead to a windfall for the director if a company is sold early in their term, the director's term will end if you sell the company, so the director will have effectively earned their equity when the company is sold.
- **D&O Insurance:** Ensure you have appropriate Directors & Officers (D&O) insurance and let new directors know the terms of the coverage. This isn't specifically part of a compensation package but is important to have in place for all directors.

For a more granular look at market data for board compensation, participate in Bolster's Board Benchmarking Study[2] for access to their tool that lets you interactively compare your data with other companies in real time.

Notes

1. Fred Wilson, "Independent Director Compensation," *AVC*, August 5, 2020, https://avc.com/2020/08/independent-director-compensation/ (accessed January 7, 2022).
2. https://bolster.com/resources/benchmark (accessed January 7, 2022).

Chapter 12

Board Diversity

While academic research on whether diverse boards lead to better company performance is mixed, the research is definitive that more diverse teams perform better and are more innovative than homogeneous teams. A recent *Harvard Business Review* article, "When and Why Diversity Improves Your Board's Performance,"[1] has a nuanced view in favor of board diversity. The authors found that diversity of thought and perspective, rather than individual diversity measures such as gender, race, or age, drive a board's success. Our perspective is that demographic measures of diversity are often drivers of diversity of thought and perspective, so pursuing an agenda of building a more diverse board gets you both benefits.

Unconscious Bias

Accepting the status quo is often default behavior in business. Unfortunately, that won't help you add diversity to your board. Wendy Lea (Energize Colorado, CEO) points out that "most founders are men and most investors are men," which results in a self-referential good-old-boys network problem unless you make a proactive effort to do something different. While this dynamic is shifting, as more new founders and VCs are female and/or coming from historically underrepresented populations, it'll take time. While the bias that comes from homogeneous boards may be unconscious, there's a cost associated with lower performance and creativity. For example, in surveys, as many as 80% of startup women think diversity offers better problem solving and improves innovation. Yet only 60% of the startup men felt the same. In contrast, 80% of men felt that they addressed diversity in the workplace, but only 60% of women agreed. That 20% gap on both those counts indicates unconscious bias.[2]

Cindy Padnos (Illuminate Ventures, Managing Partner) gives a straightforward example. While serving on a startup board, adding a new board member came up. This board was a male-dominated board, with Cindy being the lone female board member. Board members proposed several candidates, all men. Cindy recommended the name of a well-qualified woman, who the rest of the board members readily agreed was the best target candidate, and she was recruited to join the board. According to Cindy, "There was no intentional bias—it was more of a top-of-the-mind issue. Everyone readily agreed to bring her on, but no one, including the other board members who knew her better than me, thought of adding her or adding any other woman candidate."

Unconscious bias sneaks into many different decisions, with gender diversity on boards simply being one of them. Working hard to eliminate unconscious bias as an entrepreneur and board member will make your business stronger. We aren't talking about diversity for the sake of parity on some characteristics, but rather improving the quality and increasing the performance of your board. Putting someone on your board for diversity's sake isn't a solution—it just allows you to say, "We have a diverse board." But if diverse voices aren't heard and integrated into the board, you won't achieve the benefits of diversity.

Importantly, diversity isn't limited to gender. In the past few years, racial diversity, or the lack of it, has become an important topic in entrepreneurship in the US. As with efforts around increasing gender diversity, which preceded it by several years, there are now numerous efforts to increase racial diversity, both on boards and entrepreneurship in general. For boards, adding independent board members from diverse backgrounds, such as women and people of color, is a powerful way to make progress.

A boardroom filled with gender and racial diversity is a powerful signal to your leadership team, employees, and customers. Regardless of your current board's size and composition, you'll have to have an open and deliberate conversation about the topic to bring diversity to your board.

Many challenges around discussing diversity may arise, especially if your board hasn't had any formal diversity training. Phrases like "We don't want to lower the bar" or "We have a meritocracy and don't want to add a diverse candidate instead of the best candidate" are classic examples of bias that inhibit open conversations and are indications that the existing board would benefit from diversity training. As a CEO, if this is important to you throughout your company, you should include the board in your diversity training activity.

If your existing board isn't diverse, following is a two-step process for adding diverse directors to your board.

The First Step: Appoint Independent Directors Early

Matt was shocked when he reviewed the results of Bolster's first Board Benchmark study in early 2021 to find that only 33% of the companies who participated in the study had any independent directors on their boards. It was even more surprising that only 67% of the Series C or Series D companies had any independent directors. And yet, nearly every company who responded to the survey had at least one unfilled independent director seat.

Many first-time founders fear the loss of control that occurs when appointing an independent director, but as a general rule, the value a good independent director brings to a board far outweighs the risk that director poses to a founder. Adding one or more independent directors early also allows CEOs to build more diverse boards from the beginning.

The Second Step: Open Your Search to Board-Ready First-Timers

As with hiring executives, the best way to ensure that you end up with a diverse board over time is to widen the top of the funnel of candidates. To do this, you'll need to be willing to appoint board members who have never served on a board before.

The single biggest stumbling block we have heard throughout our careers is the near-universal requirement from CEOs who say, "I only want board members who have previously been a CEO or served on a board." If that's your requirement, you can almost be certain that most of your available talent pool for independent directors will be largely White and male, or that you'll simply add more board seats to the relatively few women and people of color who already serve as independent directors instead of expanding the talent pool.

It's often the case that people who haven't been CEOs or had prior board experience will bring different and equally valuable experience, skills, and perspectives to your board. If you feel you need a more experienced CEO on the board, that's a good argument for adding multiple independent directors. This may be a conversation you need to have with the rest of your board before starting a director search. Suppose someone makes a point about a first-time director "lowering the bar" for talent. In that case, you'll need to be firm in redirecting the conversation and explaining that the best independent directors had their first board seat once upon a time.

If you're relatively young or a first-time CEO, you may not want to train, or feel capable of training, someone on how to be an effective board member. However, if experienced board members are already on the board, they can help with this process.

Being "board-ready" can mean a number of things. When Bolster helps a company hire a first-time board member, it defines corporate board readiness as having done any of the following:

- having served on the board of a nonprofit, community, academic, or civic organization;
- having reported to the CEO of a company and in that capacity observed or reported in at a large number of board meetings;
- having advised many CEOs either informally or formally through an advisory board or an accelerator like Techstars;
- having participated in a meaningful corporate board education program.

Cristina Miller, Matt's first independent director at Bolster, is a great example of a first-time board member who was "board ready" without previously serving on a board. Cristina is a 10+ year senior executive who has had leadership roles at multiple marketplace companies, reporting to CEOs and spending a lot of time in board meetings. While she'd never been on a corporate board before Bolster's, she immediately added a tremendous amount of knowledge of the marketplace business. She engaged substantively both with Matt's overall strategy and in specific functional areas of the business in which Matt and team and the rest of the board had less experience. As an industry expert, Cristina has been tremendously useful, from the early stages, in helping drive product-market fit while educating the team on critical metrics to pay attention to from her prior experience.

In a post titled "We Aren't Going to Increase Diversity in the Boardroom Unless We're Willing to Appoint First-Timers. Why Is That So Hard to Do?" Heidi Roizen (Threshold Ventures, Partner) wrote about the first-time director conundrum: [3]

This to me is like saying, "I'd like to get married, but I'm optimizing for someone who has already been married because I don't want this whole marriage experience to be new to them." Look, I sort of get it—having myself been a director for dozens of public and private companies over the last 25 years (I serve on two public boards and four private boards right now). I understand there is an art and skill to being a board member. But should that be the top criterion? I believe that smart, capable people can learn what it takes to be a good board member very quickly, especially if they are onboarded properly and mentored through the process . . . We treat board service like it is some magical, secret, and superior skill set that only a rarified few can accomplish. We act as if the risk is simply too great letting a newbie into our hallowed halls. And, yes, there is skill and knowledge particular to doing a good job as a board member. But I believe that if you are already an experienced, accomplished business executive, it is just not that hard for you to learn how to be a good director.

Heidi Roizen (Threshold Ventures, Partner)

If you are committed to increasing the diversity of your board, you have to stand behind that commitment with a willingness to involve and mentor first-time directors or lean on other board members to help with that process. At some point, every single experienced board member alive today at one time had never previously served on a board before serving on their first one.

Notes

1. Stephanie J. Creary, Mary-Hunter ("Mae") McDonnell, Sakshi Ghai, and Jared Scruggs, "When and Why Diversity Improves Your Board's Performance," *Harvard Business Review*, March 27, 2019. https://hbr.org/2019/03/when-and-why-diversity-improves-your-boards-performance (accessed January 7, 2022).
2. Level Playing Field Institute, "The Tilted Playing Field: Hidden Bias in Information Technology Workplaces," 2011. www.tilted_playing_field_lpfi_9_29_11.pdf (smash.org) (accessed March 3, 2022).
3. Heidi Roizen, "We Aren't Going to Increase Diversity in the Boardroom Unless We're Willing to Appoint First-Timers. Why Is That So Hard to Do?," *Medium,* July 27, 2020. https://heidiroizen.medium.com/we-arent-going-to-increase-diversity-in-the-boardroom-unless-we-re-willing-to-appoint-first-timers-b0e456c6f8ab (accessed January 14, 2022).

Chapter 13

Onboarding Your Directors

When you add someone to your board, the CEO, along with one of the existing board members, should take responsibility for onboarding the new board member. New board members should be familiar with the legal structure and capitalization of the company, understand the current business model, and be up-to-speed on the status of the company.

Using Employee Onboarding as a Guide

The hiring process in companies doesn't end on the employee's first day—it usually extends for at least 90 days. This should be true for new board members. Take their onboarding as seriously as you take the hiring process for any employee.

If you have a structured and rigorous hiring process, you'll have done a few important things before the new director's first official board meeting, including meeting with you and other board members at least once. Your new board member will have met with several members of your executive team and attended a board meeting as an active observer.

Foundry partner and long-time CEO, Chris Moody, emphasizes setting up a new director for success. "Make sure the new board member is familiar with the financials before attending their first official board meeting. Spend time walking them through the financials line-by-line. Don't just review the board deck in advance, but allow them to ask basic questions before the first meeting."

Onboarding New Directors

Following are specific activities to onboard a new director:

- **Give the New Director a "Board Buddy:"** The "Board Buddy" is a fellow non-executive director who will immediately respond to the new director and answer any questions about the company. This can be especially helpful if a new director doesn't want to bother the CEO with board process or style issues. If your board is small or has several first-time directors, the Board Buddy could be a board observer if the observer is an experienced director.
- **Get 1:1s Scheduled:** Make sure your new director has a one-on-one meeting with every senior executive on your team. Building these relationships will help the new director understand multiple perspectives on the company and extend the director's impact on the organization.
- **Get in the Weeds with Them:** Besides reviewing financials, you, your CFO, or your general counsel should spend time familiarizing the new director with the legal structure, capitalization, financials, and current business model. If your new director is a first-time or inexperienced director, have them spend some time with your general counsel getting governance training and understanding a director's fiduciary duties.
- **Prepare an Onboarding Package:** Compile a standard board-orientation package with org charts, bios for the management team and the other directors, contact information, and past board packages.
- **Encourage In-Person Interaction:** If possible, invite the director to spend a day at the company's office, wandering around, meeting other employees, and attending an executive team meeting or all-hands meeting. This interaction can be done remotely, especially if your company has a hybrid work environment.

- **Touch Base Periodically:** Check in with the new director after each of the first few board meetings to get feedback on you, the company, and each board meeting. During these check-ins, give the director feedback on how they are showing up and make sure they understand your critical issues. Confirm they don't have any lingering questions or outstanding issues.

These check-ins will help your new board member get up-to-speed on the business. By taking board onboarding as seriously as you take your executive onboarding process, you'll derive more value from the new director and future board meetings.

Interacting with Your Team

As part of new director onboarding, clearly define how you'd like the director to interact with members of your executive team. Some CEOs prefer an hourglass model, where all communications between directors and team members run through, or include, the CEO. Others. including Matt, encourage directors and executives to have regular interactions without including the CEO, except for post-meeting summaries.

Whatever model you follow, define the rules of engagement with new board members and your executive team. If a board member disagrees with your desired approach, discuss it, and agree on an approach that works for both of you.

Chapter 14

Removing a Board Member

While there are many great board members, Mahendra identified three archetypes of difficult board members in his latest book, *The Business of Venture Capital: The Art of Raising a Fund, Structuring Investments, Portfolio Management, and Exits* (Ramsinghani, 2020).

The first is the authoritative pit bull. They dominate all meetings, treat everyone as subordinate or inferior, and perpetually demand higher sales revenues and lower burn rates. The pit bull creates a culture of fear.

Next up is the disengaged and over-stretched super-busy person. Not reading the board package or being prepared is their norm. It's unclear, from their questions, if they even understand what the company is doing. And this happens on the inconsistent occasions when they show up for a scheduled meeting.

Somewhere between the over-stretched director and the pit bull sits the passive-aggressive board member. It's never clear what they are thinking. Whispers, second-guessing, and side conversations are their favorite communication styles. You often don't realize they are manipulating you.

There are many other kinds of challenging board members. If you run a company long enough, there will almost certainly come a time when you want or need to remove a board member. Even though it is difficult, it is possible to replace a director. The approach varies depending on whether the board member is a founder, investor, or independent director.

Removing a Founder Director

The CEO of a company is almost always on the board. If a founder/CEO hires a new CEO, the founder often stays on the board, which is usually desirable, sometimes critical to the company's success, and occasionally impossible to avoid. If the founder is also on the management team reporting to the new CEO, this dynamic creates the challenge we discussed in Chapter 7, which can be managed. Still, it can lead to the founder being asked to leave the board when it generates unhealthy tension. In this situation, you can offer the founder a board observer seat to participate in the board meeting, except for the executive session.

Some early-stage companies with larger founding teams will have multiple founders on the board. As the company grows and adds investors to the board, it's good to replace the non-CEO founder-director with an independent director. As with the above situation, you can still offer the founder a board observer seat. If you are a group of founders just starting a company and put multiple founders on the initial board, talk about this openly at the beginning so this isn't a surprise when it eventually comes up.

Removing an Investor Director

Investor directors are by far the hardest to remove since they have put money into the company and likely have their board seat secured through a Voting Agreement among the stockholders. However, it's not an impossible task. Here are the critical components of the process you'll want to go through.

First, gather a lot of data. Begin by speaking confidentially to all your other board members or performing a comprehensive, professionally facilitated board 360 evaluation process. Numerous organizations run these, including Reboot, NASDAQ, Equilar, Diligent, and Bolster.[1] Ultimately, you need to make sure you have a strong and cohesive point of view across the other directors that the company would be best served by removing the investor in question from the board.

Second, identify the path forward that you'd like to pursue. Is it to replace the director with someone else at their VC firm? If so, who? Or, would you rather replace them with an independent director? Would you be okay with the VC designating an independent director, but one who sits in the VC firm's seat?

Ideally, you could have a direct conversation with the director you'd like to have leave the board. Alternatively, you could do this with your lead director or ask your lead director to initiate the conversation. Recognize that these are sensitive conversations that are difficult to have quickly and rarely resolve in the first discussion. Being open and direct while staying calm and empathetic is generally the best approach.

Suppose the situation is untenable, or you simply don't believe you or your lead director can have a constructive conversation with the director. In that case, you should work with your lead director to approach a senior partner at the investor's VC firm. This going-behind-the-back of the investor director is incredibly delicate and has to be handled with care. In addition to being candid about your feedback, offer as elegant a path forward as you can so the senior partner has several clear options.

What you're doing in this meeting is a big ask and has the potential to backfire if the senior partner disagrees, doesn't hear your feedback, or is part of a firm with a culture at odds with the feedback you are providing. You are doing more than just making a request since you'll have to communicate something back to your existing investor director, who will know that you went behind their back. The communication around this will vary widely. If you have the support of your lead director, and they're respected by the senior partner at the VC firm, that will help a lot.

VCs will generally be unwilling to give up their legal board rights, but they will be willing to consider different approaches to the request. Recently, early-stage directors have been willing to agree, in the financing documents, to leave the board after the next financing. This mechanism of having the investor board seat terminate in the next financing is another approach to consider. If your company is performing well, you'll have more options.

Removing an Independent Director

There are many reasons a board might want to remove an independent director. The person could be disruptive, fit any archetypes described, or be too busy to show up or engage. They might have a limited number of pieces of advice, and even if their pearls of wisdom are real, by the third time you've heard them and garnered nothing else from that director, you know you're past the point of diminishing returns. That's not so fun if they are three-quarters into a four-year board term.

Unlike firing a senior executive, you don't have to come to a difficult conversation with the director armed to the teeth with feedback, specifics, and an HR person in tow. Instead, you should have a reason for your decision that's understandable. However, you don't have to give a specific reason if it's negative about the person's engagement or behavior. This is a case where a statement that "the board would like to go in a different direction," or "we've had a great run getting the benefit of your expertise and want to bring someone else on now with a new set of experiences" could be the best option.

You want to take a gentle and gracious approach since the director is likely an industry influencer of some kind. You'll want to maintain a friendly and constructive relationship after they have left the board. An economic approach to soften the blow is to accelerate some or all of the director's equity grants. Or, consider giving the departing director a long Post-Termination Exercise Period (PTEP), so they don't have to write a check to exercise their options immediately.

Ideally, if you had set up a predefined board term of service that was one or two years instead of four, you'd have an easier time if things weren't working out, since, in your worst case, you wouldn't have that long to wait until the end of the director's service and then not renew them for a subsequent term. This is another argument for shorter board terms.

Getting Rid of the Entire Board

As successful as Apple may be, its boardroom dynamics were complicated. When Apple's board brought back Steve Jobs after almost going bankrupt, Steve immediately started to work his ways. He didn't respect his board and bluntly said, "This company is in shambles and I don't have time to wet-nurse the board. So I need all of you to resign. Or else I am going to resign and not come back on Monday."[2] After the board resigned, Jobs brought in Larry Ellison, founder of Oracle, who hated meetings and came to only a third of the board meetings. Jobs had a life-size cardboard cutout picture of Larry put in. Over the years, Jobs brought strong people onto Apple's board, including Al Gore, Eric Schmidt of Google, and Bill Campbell of Intuit. Then, Google decided to develop Android, which competed directly with the iPhone. Jobs famously lost his temper, banished Eric Schmidt from the Apple board, and went on a warpath against Google and Android.

Biographer Walter Isaacson writes, "He always made sure they were loyal to a fault. Despite their stature, they seemed at times awed or intimidated by Jobs, and were eager to keep him happy." Jobs even invited the former Chairman of the SEC, Arthur Levitt, but then found that Arthur was a huge proponent of strong and independent boards. Jobs promptly uninvited him, saying that Levitt's views didn't apply to Apple's culture.

Getting rid of your entire board may sound like a good idea, especially during a dark moment when you are particularly frustrated with your board, but it's unlikely you'll be able to pull this off in a VC-backed startup. We know of an example where a CEO, whom the board discussed replacing, tried to fire the entire board. "He honestly thought he could terminate the board as he had raised the money and knew the various shareholders. The siren songs in his own head started to play and he thought he could do it all," says a VC who served on this board. Ultimately, the board fired the CEO.

Notes

1. https://bolster.com/resources/how-to-evaluate-your-board (accessed January 8, 2022).
2. Walter Isaacson, *Steve Jobs* (New York: Simon & Schuster, 2011), pp. 318–319.

Chapter 15

Is an Advisory Board Useful?

Advisory boards can be a great source of help for entrepreneurs. They can also be valuable for people who want to understand and become involved in startups. But they are very different from a board of directors.

Some startups attract industry luminaries as advisors and then showcase them as an advisory board. Beyond the recognition of a well-known person on your website, an advisory board can help you navigate the tricky waters of an early-stage startup, attract your first customer, develop your product, execute a financing, recruit critical people, or resolve issues with your co-founders.

While advisory boards have potential, they can be incredibly frustrating for all involved. It's essential to understand the difference so that you don't recruit the wrong people for, or get the wrong things from, the wrong board.

The guidance from an advisory board member may be similar to a board member, but there are some differences between them. While advisory board members provide coaching, industry insights, access to people who can be helpful to the business, and credibility, they don't have a responsibility or duty to act in the interest of all shareholders. Unlike the board of directors, the advisory board doesn't meet formally, have any control rights, or have typical director legal responsibilities such as "duty of care" and "duty of loyalty" (see Table 15.1). Advisory boards infrequently meet, and many advisory board member relationships are ad-hoc, one-on-one interactions when desired by the CEO.

Table 15.1   How an advisory board differs from a board of directors

	Board of directors	Advisory board
Appointed by	Investors and shareholders	CEO and founders
Engagement	Formally defined in financing documents	Defined by the CEO as needed
Duties	Bound by formal duty of care and loyalty	Bound by simple confidentiality agreement
Actions	Proactive and hands-on, can fire the CEO	Reactive and supportive
Term	Defined	Can be permanent or fluid
Responsibility	To all shareholders	To the CEO, CTO, or founders
Interests	High with financial, reputational, legal, and career risks	Low with little or no skin in the game

As Steve Blank noted:

At the end of the day, your board is not your friend. You may like them and they might like you, but they have a fiduciary duty to the shareholders, not the founders. And they have a fiduciary responsibility to their own limited partners. That means the board is your boss, and they have an obligation to optimize results for the company. You may be the ex-employee one day if they think you're holding the company back.[1]

In contrast, the advisory board can be your friend, as they don't have any fiduciary responsibilities or formal duties.

Board of Directors vs. Advisory Board

Many first-time founders receive the advice to have a "board of advisors" at the beginning and avoid forming a board of directors early on. However, we believe the formality of a board of directors helps founders because it creates an additional level of commitment from the directors. It's easy to be an advisor since there's no formal commitment or legal responsibility to the company. However, directors suddenly have magical "fiduciary duties" that, while they rarely come into play, increase the seriousness of the role.

Many entrepreneurs don't want to be hassled by a board of directors early on. Consequently, we've heard excuses ranging from a fear of losing control of the company, to not wanting to be responsible to a board, or not wanting to waste time communicating with board members. We think these are classic errors in thinking about the role of the early-stage board. The job of a great early-stage board member is to reinforce CEOs' and entrepreneurs' success. A board member's contribution can take many forms and styles, but fundamentally it's a support role, and entrepreneurs now have another high-powered person on their team.

While a board of directors is essential to startups, there's a role for an advisory board. An advisory board can be a trial board approach before creating a board of directors so that you can "try before you buy." And a board of advisors can be tremendously helpful to startups and scaleups—if you do it right.

Attributes of a Useful Advisory Board Member

Some useful advisory board member attributes overlap with a good board member, but there are numerous differences. Some follow:

- **Ability to Complement the Formal Board Member and Investor Skills and Mindset:** Advisory board members must understand that they play a different role than board members.
- **Long-term Commitment:** Creating a successful company takes a long time. While advisory board members can have a short-term impact, they're much more effective if they have a long-term view of the company's development.
- **Creative Thinking:** The CEO and leadership team members need as much creative input as they can get. While some of this can come from the board of directors, the dynamics between the board and a CEO can limit it. An advisory board member can be a source of out-of-the-box thinking.
- **Responsiveness:** Rapid response is critical. CEOs will be looking for specific help from advisory board members. Responses beyond a few days will be useless.
- **Emotional Stability and Positive Attitude:** The CEO already has enough pressure. The advisory board can be a safe, comfortable place for the CEO to explore specific issues and get direct advice and feedback.

- **Can Invest Some Cash in the Company and Have Skin in the Game:** Mark Suster (Upfront Ventures, Partner) writes in his blog, "Even getting $10,000 out of someone who's already a millionaire and super-successful gets you emotional buy-in. Therefore you're more likely to get value."[2]

Selecting Advisory Board Members

In his book, *The Four Steps to the Epiphany*, Steve Blank (2013) suggests a startup should recruit five different kinds of advisory board members at various stages of a company's evolution.

1. *Technical*: Offers product development advice.
2. *Business*: Offers business strategy guidance.
3. *Customer*: Offers direction on product features/value proposition.
4. *Industry*: Brings domain expertise.
5. *Sales*: Counsels on sales tactics and demand creation.

In cases where your investors have little or no domain knowledge about certain aspects of your business, an advisory board can be a huge asset.

Building an Advisory Board

Here's a way to approach building an advisory board:

- **State a Clear Purpose:** Figure out what kind of advisory board you want to build. Does it function as a group, or is it a collection of individual advisors and a board in name only?
- **Manage Expectations:** Clarify the mission, role, and expected time required from advisors on paper, both for yourself and the people you ask.
- **Pay Something:** Be prepared to pay for people's time, almost always with a stock option grant. These grants should be significantly smaller than the grants you give your independent directors, typically in the range of 0.1% to 0.25% vesting over four years.

- **Staff the Bench Deliberately:** Figure out whom you want on your advisory board upfront, along with a few people in reserve. You may want a financial advisor, an industry advisor, a seasoned CEO to act as a mentor or coach, and a technical advisor. Think this through, but make sure you have a bench.
- **Aim High:** Seek out accomplished founders and executives. People will be flattered. Many will say yes. The worst is they'll decline and refer you to others who might be similarly helpful.
- **Keep up Communications:** Make sure you include your advisory board in enough company communications so they are up-to-speed and can be helpful when you need them.

Challenges of Advisory Boards

While an advisory board can be helpful, it can also have dysfunctional dynamics, either at the specific advisor level or the overall advisory board level. Advisors might be excellent contributors as individuals but not fully integrated functioning groups. Scott Banister (IronPort Systems, Co-founder) says:

> At IronPort, we had advisors but not an advisory board. One advisor actually came to most board meetings despite having no seat, observer or otherwise. Another provided management and HR advice to the CEO. And we encouraged executives to have their own advisors as well. I think this works better than thinking of them as a board of any sort.

Advisory board members will have different levels of individual engagement. Make sure your expectations are well defined and shared by the advisory board members. Many advisors sign up with immense enthusiasm, only to vanish after signing their stock option agreement. Be clear on expectations, time commitments, and how you measure the advisory member's contribution. Ideally, this would be written in a formal offer, similar to that of any employee or service provider, and be agreed to by the advisor.

Make sure you understand any conflicts in advance. Great advisors will often be engaged with multiple startups. The commitments can generate conflicts concerning time, attention, or confidentiality. Advisors who function with high integrity will maintain confidentiality and respect your ideas, while others will be less careful. You must understand these conflicts before you sign them up.

Some CEOs throw a small number of options at many advisors, hoping that the advisors will take their call or refer talent and customers to the company. A more effective approach is to have a small number of advisors who are deeply committed to the company and are proactive, intentional, and systematic in putting their talents to use for you and your team.

You have many competing priorities. While having an advisory board may be helpful, make sure you're committed to spending the time to cultivate and maintain the relationships. In the absence of your attention, the advisory board will probably turn into a list of names on your website with no discernible impact on your company. If you don't manage your advisory board, you'll get no value from it. But when it goes well, it can be immensely beneficial.

Notes

1. Steve Blank, "Don't Give Away Your Board Seats," *WSJ*, June 13, 2013. https://www.wsj.com/articles/BL-232B-1051 (accessed January 14, 2022).
2. Mark Suster, "Should Your Startup Have an Advisory Board?," *Both Sides*, October 12, 2009. http://www.bothsidesofthetable.com/2009/10/12/should-your-startup-have-an-advisory-board/ (accessed January 14, 2022).

Section 3

Preparing for and Running the Board Meeting

Chapter 16

Preparing for the Board Meeting

"**Y**ou have received their investment—now stop selling, please," says Eric Jensen. "CEOs often start their first board meeting as if they are making an investor pitch—sharing how great their company is, how big the market is, and describing the vision. This is no longer necessary. The investors are now in the boat and it's time to start rowing with their help."

A typical board meeting runs from one to four hours, depending upon the agenda and frequency of meetings. The meeting starts with the chair calling the meeting to order, followed by the CEO providing an update on the business and a summary of key metrics. The CFO provides a financial update. The VP of Sales walks through the previous quarter's performance and the upcoming quarter's pipeline. The VP of Engineering demonstrates key features in the next release, and the VP of Marketing reviews the launch plans. After the updates, the board tackles substantive issues, typically covering one to three big topics. The board is interactive, asking questions while providing guidance and real-time feedback during the discussion. At the end of the meeting, all observers and management other than the CEO leave for an Executive Session where the CEO and the board can speak freely. A Closed Session where the CEO steps out and the board discusses the progress, any concerns that have arisen, and any feedback for the CEO follows the Executive Session. The chair then follows up with the CEO to discuss anything that came up in the Closed Session.

The Value of Preparation

As with any group or team meeting, the better the preparation, the more effective the meeting. Since your board only meets a few times a year, preparation is critical to orient directors to the details, context, current state of your business, and issues you face. Your board members have other jobs (often full-time). VC directors can sit on a dozen boards at once. When Brad first joined the board of Return Path, he was on over 30 other boards, which was ludicrous with the benefit of hindsight. Thorough preparation helps a director engage effectively.

While the board meeting may be the main event, preparing for the board meeting can be at least half the value of the experience. If taken seriously, preparation creates significant alignment between all leadership team members, surfaces ambiguities, and focuses on key issues where the team and the CEO need feedback.

While a board meeting can be an intense 24-hour period, especially if there is a board dinner, travel, and inclusion of the entire leadership team, the preparation is often longer. The preparation includes several days of intense work: meetings, spreadsheets, documents, and soul-searching. If you do this prep work, you and your team will have already gotten a huge benefit out of the process.

Pulling materials together is one thing—crafting the overall story is entirely different. The board meeting gives you a chance to step back from the daily grind of running the business and think about what's been going on and where you are going as a business. Instead of being buried in work, you'll spend time focusing on the core issues facing the business. Rather than dealing with the daily barrage of tactics and decisions, you'll spend time with your team on strategy, competitive dynamics, and what you need to do to create value in the business. By writing it down, presenting it to the board, and discussing it as a group, you'll generate deep alignment on where you are heading and what you need to do to get there.

The Meeting Agenda

Develop and publish the meeting agenda in advance of the meeting. Lee Mayer (founder and CEO of Havenly) notes how the agenda evolved and became more useful as she gained experience.

> *In our first board meetings I had a 60–70-page deck with very detailed data on the business because I wanted board members to be informed on what we were doing and planning. But I learned that the board consumes whatever you put in front of it and board members would drill down deep into information that wasn't necessarily strategic to what we were thinking about, and the meeting wouldn't be very guided or productive. Now I provide two decks—a "background deck" that provides quarterly data and department metrics and updates so board members are informed, and a shorter, "strategic discussion deck" that contains relevant information around topics I want to address. I set the expectation that board members should review the background deck in advance, but I want their thinking on the strategic deck in the meeting. This has made our board meeting focused and more productive.*

A good board meeting agenda addresses the most critical issues, focusing on the strategic issues facing the business. Business updates should be covered in advance of the meeting in the board package. Reviewing the business should take at most 30 minutes of the actual meeting, with the bulk of the meeting spent discussing the strategic issues. While 80% of the board book might be a business review or retrospective, only 20% of the time in the meeting should focus on these things.

Many startup CEOs front-load the agenda with updates and push strategic discussions to the end of the meeting. When there isn't a focus on the key issues or a weak agenda, the meeting drifts and suddenly board members have to rush to catch their flights or drop from the videoconference to go to their next meeting. Consequently, in this loose agenda meeting, the most important items don't get adequate attention, which is a recurring flaw. In a

McKinsey study of 586 corporate directors, respondents pointed out that they would like to double their time on strategic discussions.[1]

Focus on Critical Items

Rather than get caught up in the day-to-day details of the business, use your board to address key strategic challenges. Is your business model changing? Do you have a key partnership that can make or break the business? When do you need a new round of financing? Are you struggling with scaling your leadership team? Is an exogenous issue threatening the survival of your company?

Regularly ask directors before the meeting if they'd like you to explore specific topics. Be open to this even after you've sent out the board materials, as this may change the focus of parts of the board meeting. By hearing what directors want to discuss ahead of time, you won't be surprised if one goes deep on an issue during the meeting that you previously weren't planning to discuss.

Conflicts between management team members, specific board members, or management and the board are important to address in Executive Session or Closed Session. "Use the executive sessions as an opportunity to understand the issue deeper. Ask probing questions, in a non-confrontational manner. Don't judge the response, use active listening to better grasp management's position and strategy," says Padmasree Warrior (founder and CEO of Fable, Board member, Microsoft and Spotify).

You'll be more effective if you master the basis of conflict. In the book, *Crucial Conversations: Tools for Talking When Stakes Are High*,[2] the authors offer a set of tools that anyone can use to handle conflict in an adult manner, including:

- *Commit to Seek Mutual Purpose*: We all want this company to be successful.
- *Recognize the Purpose Behind Their Strategy*: You aren't satisfied with this situation or outcome and wish to do something about it. I understand your position.
- *Invent a Mutual Purpose*: When we get past this situation, our company can be stronger.

- *Brainstorm New Strategies*: How about we focus on a different approach A or a different approach B instead of the current approach C that we disagree on?

Tim Miller suggests, "If you are uncertain on how to approach a problem, start one-on-one with a key board member." Rather than making assertions or asking vague, open-ended questions, frame the issues as hypotheses. For example,

- Here's a problem, and I don't know the answer. Can you give me some insights on where to start?
- Here's what I want to do. Tell me if I am wrong and give me constructive feedback.
- I've decided, and I want to get your views, especially if you think I'm missing something.

The Board Book

The board book, which is a combination of an agenda and comprehensive report, is the document that will organize and direct your meetings. A good board book provides all the context and information before the board meeting. As Martina Lauchengo (Partner at Costanoa Ventures) says, "Your board's ability to provide helpful advice depends on how you frame conversations. Make sure your board book elicits discussion and doesn't just report out."

Be deliberate and thoughtful about what you put in the board book. Following are a few tips:

- **Use a Consistent Format for the Board Book for All Board Meetings:** While you'll evolve the content of the board book, board members come to think of it like a newspaper or magazine they read regularly. When they compare it to the board book from the previous quarter, it's easier to navigate.
- **Publish the Core Board Book in a Single PDF:** Combine all the material, including the cover memo, spreadsheets, reports, memos, and presentations in one document. Then, combine them into a single PDF. Then, when it's all compiled into a single PDF, number the pages in the PDF.[3]

- **Separate Third-Party Reference Documents:** You may have several other documents, including: (1) third-party documents such as audits or valuations, (2) board or shareholder resolutions, noting that signatures will be collected electronically after the meeting, and/or (3) confidential memos for the Executive Session. While your core meeting materials are in one document, send these out separately. When they are for directors' eyes only, send them only to board members.

- **Use a Collaborative Workspace for the Documents:** Rather than emailing the documents around, consider having an invite-only collaborative workspace for them, such as Google Drive. It's still useful to have the core document compiled into a PDF, but if it is also in a Google Doc, board members can comment directly in the document and ask questions between receiving the materials and the actual meeting. Ideally, the management team has access to the document and can respond to questions from the board. This tactic reduces the number of questions about the material in the board meeting and allows you to focus on strategic issues, rather than getting board members up to speed and answering questions about the materials.

There are many different styles of board books. Some are short (less than 20 pages), while others can be 100 or more pages long. Some are in document format, while others are in presentation format. The following are two examples.

Board Book Example: Matt's Board Book

Matt uses a written format for his board book. He started with a series of memos early in the life of Return Path and evolved it over time to a comprehensive document that was consistent from board meeting to board meeting. He has preserved the approach with his new company, Bolster, but has shifted to a presentation format:

1. *Cover memo:* A short (less than one page) note framing the meeting, highlighting critical discussion topics and events

since the last meeting. It includes a summary agenda and meeting logistics, including time, place, directions, dial-in/ videoconferencing links.

2. *Official business*: Another short note that covers the issues for discussion and approval as well as the relevant documents, including prior meeting minutes for approval, other resolutions for approval, stock option grants, outside valuations, audits, a financing update, any transaction updates, and a legal update.

3. *Retrospective*: A summary recapping the prior reporting period and highlighting the topics to discuss in the meeting. Financial statements and reports follow this.

These first three items will typically represent about 80% of Matt's board book material.

4. *On My Mind/Issues/Discussion Topics*: This section is the core of the meeting. It describes up to three issues on Matt's mind with a graphic showing the issues on his mind from the last meeting and which ones map forward to this meeting. Each topic has a corresponding memo written by the leadership team member who will lead the discussion. This memo includes the goals of this section, including any desired decisions.

5. *Executive Session*: If Matt has confidential issues for the closed session, there's a separate memo for this.

6. *Closed Session*: There are no materials for this section, but Matt includes it in his board book and on the agenda to make sure it happens.

Board Book Example: Rover

Brad served on Rover's board of directors from early in its life (less than ten employees) through Rover becoming a public company. During that time, Rover's board book went through several evolutions, eventually settling into one of the most effective formats that Brad has encountered.

Until they went public, Rover separated financial reporting from the board meeting by having a separate "State of the Business Update" a week before the board meeting. A detailed financial update with extensive analysis is distributed for this meeting. As a result, board meetings focus on strategy and business issues rather than a financial review.

Consequently, the agenda varies, but most of the meeting covers *Special Topics*, similar to Matt's section titled *On My Mind/Issues/Discussion Topics*. Following is an example of an agenda from a Rover board meeting.

Executive Update/Minutes—15 minutes

Governance & Org—15 minutes

Special Topics

> International Update—10 minutes
>
> Context—10 minutes
>
> Next Year's Budget—1.5 hours
>
> Long-Range Cash Proposal—20 minutes

Full Board Wrap-up—20 minutes

While Aaron Easterly (Rover's CEO) doesn't enforce the time bounds rigidly, he uses them to keep things moving. For perspective on the consistency of the agenda, here is one from another meeting.

Governance & Organization Update—30 minutes

Special Topics

> Fundraise & Liquidity Update—15 minutes
>
> Update on Potential Acquisition of Company X—
> 15 minutes
>
> Marketing Philosophy, US & Intl—30 minutes
>
> International Expansion—30 minutes
>
> Second Headquarters/Alternate Location—30 minutes

Executive/Private Session—30 minutes

At the beginning of each section is a simple slide that frames the discussion with the question, "This section will be a success if . . ." For example:

Section Title

This section will be a success if . . .

Board approves xyz

Board agrees with continued approach to abc

Discussion ensues on fundraise update

By spending 60 seconds going through this slide before each section, the board aligns on what Aaron and the leadership team are looking to accomplish.

Sending Out the Board Book

Send out the board book at least three days before the board meeting. Matt believes it's more important to give directors a weekend plus a business day than a set number of days. Using his approach, you'll always send the board book out on the Friday before the following week's board meeting, although if the board book is short because you're an early-stage company, the three-day rule suffices. Regardless of your approach, give the directors plenty of time to review the board material in advance, so they have no excuse for coming to the meeting unprepared.

Creating an Annual Calendar

Create an annual calendar for the next year during the current year's fourth quarter. While it might seem tedious to schedule things for an entire year, your board members, especially your investors who may serve on a dozen boards, have jam-packed calendars. Try to schedule meetings through January of the year following next year.

The frequency of meetings varies based on the stage of a company, but you should have at least one meeting per quarter. Mark Suster says, "Most startups have meetings much more frequently, sometimes as often as once a month. Things change so quickly, and investors also don't understand your business well enough in the beginning. In two months, a lot can change in a pure startup."[4]

Many companies have a periodic meeting that's an abbreviated board meeting. Often called an "Operational Update," this is an operational and financial review for the board. While it's considered a formal meeting, the scope is limited to just the operational details agreed in advance.

An example is an eight meetings per year tempo, with quarterly board meetings plus a quarterly Operational Update in-between each board meeting. Another approach would be a monthly financial review meeting separate from the quarterly board meetings.

Regardless of your approach, be consistent, and schedule all the meetings a year in advance.

Notes

1. *McKinsey Quarterly*, "Survey on Governance." www.mckinsey.com. February 2008. Of the 586 respondents, 378 were privately held companies, making it a relevant sample for the purposes of our discussion.
2. K. Patterson, J. Grenny, R. McMillan, and A. Switzler, *Crucial Conversations* (New York: McGraw Hill, 2002).
3. A simple Adobe Macro can do this. See https://drive.google.com/file/d/1YKob9Cf6LJAYC8RfKzaghJiwUQrwRZqE/view.
4. Mark Suster, "Running More Effective Board Meetings at Startups," *Both Sides*, February 12, 2010, http://www.bothsidesofthetable.com/2010/02/12/running-more-effective-board-meetings-at-startups/ (accessed January 14, 2022).

Chapter 17

Meeting Dynamics

As the CEO, you define meeting hygiene. Do you have a culture of laptops in the meeting, or should all computers, tablets, and smartphones be put away? Is checking email in the meeting acceptable? Is there a five-minute break every hour, or should people just get up and go to the bathroom when they need to?

For in-person meetings, food is often overlooked. Brad is a vegetarian and has been at thousands of board meetings where his only choice for something to eat was a ham sandwich and potato chips. You don't have to be extravagant, especially if you are a pre-revenue startup, but knowing your board members' food and drink preferences and putting a little effort into accommodating them sets a positive tone. In the era of GrubHub and UberEats, it's easy and inexpensive to get great food at a board meeting tailored to directors' preferences.

While it may seem trivial, you'll have a more effective meeting if everyone knows about it and operates using the same ground rules. Mutual respect will be higher as no one will be observing a different cultural norm in the meeting that will cause someone to feel disrespected.

Seating

Matt has one rule for seating during board meetings: directors have to sit together at one end of the table. Everyone else can fill in the rest of the table or side seating. While this may sound silly, Matt likes to have a lot of observers and management team members at board meetings. He believes board members have better conversations if they're at a smaller table and don't feel like they are talking across the observers or need to include all the observers in every part of the conversation.

There's a videoconference version of this rule, which is to hide participants not on video. After a few minutes of everyone saying hello at the beginning of a meeting to see who is there, you can politely ask observers and management team members to turn off their video when they aren't speaking. This limits the number of people in boxes on the screen to only the directors, resulting in a more intimate conversation. You can ask anyone to "unhide" themselves at any time to join a discussion or answer a specific question.

In contrast, Brad prefers a more chaotic version of this, where people sit wherever they want. He also prefers everyone on video, not just the directors. But, he's always been willing to conform to whatever a CEO wants. Remember, if you are the CEO, it's your meeting, and you get to define how it works.

The Meeting Length

A typical board meeting lasts from one to four hours. The lead director and the CEO ensure the meeting starts and ends on time. A highly functioning board isn't materially different from any other high-functioning team—the group needs to have clear responsibilities, clear lines of communication, and open dialog. If someone is going to be late or has difficulty with a conflict, be proactive about what is happening rather than making everyone wait.

Before or after the board meeting, dinner is a good way to enhance relationships. It can take any form: board only, board and observers, or the board and senior management. Once a year, it can be helpful and fun to do an event like bowling (the lowest common denominator of sporting activities) or a cooking class. Make sure it's an event that allows people to interact; taking your board to a theater production is a nice perk, but it won't create the social time you want. Whatever you choose, it doesn't have to be expensive, but try to incorporate social time into your board agenda. You'd never go a whole year without having a team dinner or outing, so treat your board the same way.

Including Your Team in the Board Meeting

There's substantial value in including your entire leadership team in the board meeting. While allowing team members to participate represents your opportunity to let your team shine, the board meeting isn't a feel-good social event. Rather than feeling like you need to have each team member take an active role in the meeting, let the agenda drive engagement. However, avoid filling the boardroom with too many bodies, as that can devolve into a counterproductive parade.

Giving your senior executives as much exposure to the board as possible is incredibly valuable for their career development. Your team hears from directors what's on their minds and how they think about the business, which allows you to weave board feedback into your management team discussions in an organic way.

One risk of having management team members at board meetings is that one of them seizes on a particular comment as a directive from the board as opposed to a part of a broader conversation. Matt once had to course-correct after a board meeting by having the following conversation with one of his senior leaders:

EXECUTIVE: What do you mean we aren't going to do X? Didn't you hear in the meeting when Director A said we should do that?

MATT: Yes, I did hear that, but that was part of a broader conversation about X topic that had multiple points of view.

EXECUTIVE: Right, but Director A was really adamant that we do X.

MATT: Yes, he was. But did you hear when Director B and Director C had different points of view? Our job is to take feedback from across the board, especially when there isn't clear consensus, and make the best decisions possible as the leaders of the business. In this case, X is problematic because of Y. So we are doing Z. I'll make sure to communicate that clearly to Director A.

Remind your team that the board rarely gives specific directives and is there as a general strategic sounding board. Cover any particularly contentious or confusing conversations with your team in a post-meeting debrief.

Slides or No Slides?

The default setting for most boards is to review a slide deck during the meeting. Frequently, this deck is the same that gets sent around ahead of the meeting as the board book. Matt iterated on this model over the years. Finally, he concluded that the best meetings were the ones that were entirely slide-free unless there was a compelling reason to post a single visual here or there in the meeting.

If everyone prepares for meetings with a comprehensive set of materials, the meeting can become a discussion instead of a presentation. Everyone is highly engaged. No checking email. No yawns. Nobody is nodding off. If there are slides on the wall (or on-screen), everyone looks at the slides. If there are no slides, everyone looks at each other and connects. When Matt reflects on the 20 years of Return Path, he thinks the change to slide-free board meetings was one of the most impactful things he ever did for the engagement of directors and productivity of board meetings.

Discussion or Decision Item?

Most of the topics covered in board meetings aren't ones where the board decides. During board meetings, there's often extensive discussion around a topic that results in a decision, but the decision is ultimately the responsibility of the CEO. The ambiguity of whether a topic is a discussion or decision item generates significant confusion in board meetings, especially when management is in the room, and you have forceful directors expressing their opinion.

In situations where you want the board to decide, be specific about this at the outset of the discussion. Separate this from topics where you want a deep discussion from the board but ultimately decide what to do. This is especially important in situations where board approval isn't explicitly required. Be clear when you ask your board to help you decide something instead of having a discussion to get input, but not ceding your decision to the board.[1]

The Executive Session and the Closed Session

Board meetings should always end with an Executive Session. We recommend a three-step process. First, there should be an Executive Session with all board members. Anyone not on the board other than the general counsel (observers and management team members) should leave. This session gives the board a chance to have a "closed board meeting" that also benefits from being attorney-client privileged[2] if the board needs to discuss any sensitive information.

At the end of the full board Executive Session, there should be a second Executive Session (sometimes called a Closed Session) with non-management board members. In this session, the CEO and any other management team members on the board leave. The remaining board members discuss any fundamental concerns they have about the CEO, the direction, or the company's dynamic. The lead director should facilitate this session and summarize the discussion at the end to make sure each director agrees with any conclusions or recommendations.

Finally, the lead director should meet privately with the CEO and discuss any issues from the Closed Session. This feedback should be precise, and the lead director should be careful not to editorialize.

Usually, the Executive Session will be a non-event, especially if the board's culture is to be open and direct. However, if there are leadership issues or fundamental concerns about the company or the CEO, the Executive Session creates a relatively safe environment to bring these issues up. Having a separate Executive Session after every board meeting avoids the awkwardness of calling a separate session as there is an opportunity at every board meeting to have this type of discussion.

Jeff Bussgang (Flybridge Capital Partners, General Partner) writes:

> *When I was an entrepreneur, I was initially uncomfortable with this idea of stepping out of the room so that the board could talk about me and "my company." But I came to appreciate the value of the private session for both the board and the company. It's an opportunity for the board to gain alignment on the key takeaways, direction to give the management team, and a forum to make decisions around compensation and bonuses, CEO performance feedback, financing, and generally build a functional decision-making unit.[3]*

A Board Call Instead of a Meeting

Often, board meetings happen on short notice and happen via a video or conference call instead of a physical, in-person meeting. During the height of the COVID pandemic, all meetings shifted to remote meetings, Zoom became ubiquitous, and the concept of a "board meeting" converged with a "board call," which was mostly a Zoom meeting. These different types of remote meetings, regardless of the platform (conference call, Zoom, Microsoft Teams, Google Meet, Cisco WebEx, or your own favorite video-conferencing system), are now simply called a "board call."

Occasionally, the board call is merely a periodic update. In these situations, information flows mostly from the CEO to the board. Any specific items discussed or voted on should be well framed in advance by the CEO or the lead director.

While speed and efficiency are the obvious advantages of a call, the challenges include dropped calls, lack of engagement, or rapport. Building consensus via a call has its challenges, especially around complex topics. As a result, have a tight agenda, a clear leader, and written material distributed ahead of time for a call.

If you choose to make a formal motion via a call, start with a roll call of attendees. Participants should have an opportunity to weigh in and assert their position. Ask each one formally to speak, especially those who may be silent. "Angeli, we have not heard your opinion on this. Could you share your thoughts?" If one person dominates the conversation, try saying, "Thank you for your opinion. Can we also get the others to weigh in?" Clarify each person's position with a statement such as "So, before we wrap up, let me make sure I've gotten all of your feedback."

Remote Attendees and Hybrid Meetings

When you have one or more remote attendees at a board meeting, videoconferencing is much more effective than audioconferencing. Today, all videoconferencing options include the ability for audio-only participants, so put some energy into setting up an effective video and audio system in whatever room you will use for your board meetings. Finally, test out your environment as you add new board members to make it easy and effective for them to engage remotely.

Videoconferencing changes the board dynamics dramatically. Before COVID, many CEOs insisted on in-person board meetings. If someone joined remotely, it was their responsibility to engage effectively. After COVID, you will inevitably have remote directors joining by videoconference, so it's now the CEO and lead director's responsibility to ensure that remote participants are engaged. If done correctly, it can be as effective as an in-person meeting, especially given that the entire business world had over a year of deeply remote engagement, and much of the business world is engaged in a hybrid model for the indefinite future.

Following are the primary challenges with videoconferencing:

- **A Disengaged Remote Participant:** While the entire business world now has meaningful experience with videoconferencing, many people still haven't figured out that there isn't such a thing as multitasking. While the days of in-person directors spending all the time on the BlackBerry is long over (especially since BlackBerries no longer exist in any meaningful way), most in-person meeting participants now engage fully in the meeting, rather than getting distracted by email or scrolling through their Twitter feed.

This behavior is not, however, true of many remote participants. As CEO, you can make a strong request for full attention from remote participants and, if you don't feel like you are getting it, discuss it with the participant directly after the meeting. If you are uncomfortable with this confrontation, have your lead director do it. But don't let it become a pattern, as most remote participants will acknowledge it and then change their behavior going forward.

- **A Poor In-Room Setup:** Brad has been a remote participant for most board meetings since he decided to stop traveling for work in 2013. Before that, he traveled 75% of the time but was often still a remote participant, since he'd be traveling on the East Coast and having board meetings in Boston and New York the same week that he'd have a San Francisco board meeting. Since a portable teleportation system had not yet been invented, the only way to do a morning board meeting in New York and an afternoon board meeting in San Francisco was to do one of them remotely. In 2013, there were still many poor in-room videoconferencing setups, so Brad had to become "good at remote" even if the in-room setup was inadequate. In 2022, there's no excuse for a poor in-room setup. A large TV with quality audio, video, and microphones isn't expensive and can be installed with minimal cost and AV support. Test it yourself from the perspective of a remote participant when there's a room full of people. If you can engage effectively from your laptop for three hours, you've got a good in-room setup.

- **A Leader Who Doesn't Engage Remote Participants:** While this is never an issue with a fully-remote call, it often is an issue with a hybrid call. The participants in the room get a lot of airtime and eye contact, while the hybrid participants feel like they are watching whatever is going on in the room. It's difficult or awkward to break into the discussion, and long stretches go by without anyone acknowledging or checking in with the remote participants. There's an art to a CEO managing a hybrid meeting. If it's not effective in a board setting, it's probably not effective inside the company either. As a CEO, be deliberate about how you engage in hybrid meetings, and ask for feedback from everyone, both in and out of the room, after the meeting.

Setting up rules in advance of the meeting helps with all three of these issues. Simple rules, like on-demand rather than scheduled bathroom breaks (just go, don't wait), remote participants muting when they aren't speaking (so there isn't background noise), using the in-meeting chat or raising your hand if you are remote and want to say something, and being fully engaged in the meeting (e.g., don't check email and, if you realize you are, stop and bring your attention back to the meeting) are common ones.

Remote and hybrid meetings are here to stay. They're remarkably effective and almost as good as being in the same physical space when done right. That said, it's still not quite the same. An emerging best practice is for boards to have one meeting per year in-person, including dinner and some social time, and a longer form meeting around a big topic such as annual planning, to balance out other meetings that are remote-only.

The Post-Meeting Survey

Matt recently adopted a practice recommended by Fred Wilson, a short post-meeting survey sent via Google Forms immediately after the meeting ends. It asks directors the following questions:

1. Name (Optional).
2. What are 1–3 areas/specifics where we are doing well?
3. What are 1–3 areas/specifics you're concerned about or where we could do better?
4. Did the meeting meet your objectives for learning and discussion? (Yes/No)
5. If not, why not?
6. Do you have any other feedback for Matt at this time?

This kind of survey can give you a helpful, quick read on what's in directors' heads following the meeting. It adds to any notes you share with your team and the content of the follow-up conversation you had with your lead director after the Closed Session.

Post Meeting

After the meeting, convene your leadership team and debrief the board meeting and the post-meeting survey. Discuss the entire meeting, summarize decisions, and list the next steps or clarifications required. Use this meeting to reinforce key points for your team.

Good boards appreciate that CEOs listen and follow up with feedback or clarifications. If you call a board member after the board meeting with a simple question, "I wanted to make sure I did not miss your point. Did you mean . . .?" that speaks to your ability to understand what was said.

A board member can play a meaningful role in ensuring clarity and follow-up. Meg Porfido states:

> *As chair, I typically ask the CEO, "Did you get what you wanted out of the meeting? If not, how can I help?" We sometimes decide to shift future agendas, or sometimes I can play a more proactive role and clarify or follow up with board members. As a board, we want to help; we should not be a distraction, and we should not have our own agenda. We are coming in and out of the CEO's sphere. At our best, we stay in our lane, energizing them with ideas gleaned from our own experience.*

If a board member suggests an action item, which may require searching for a simple data point or conducting an extensive evaluation, address the request. Ensure that the request is aligned with the current needs of the business, isn't arbitrary, and is actionable. Before you commit resources, make sure that other board members are aligned with the request. For example, a board member might suggest an irrelevant business action such as "Let's create a model to assess the impact of a meteor hitting the Earth." Rather than ignore it, address it with whoever requested it, calibrate the value of the request with other board members, and explicitly decide whether to do it.

Notes

1. The idea of discussion vs. decision item came from Seth Levine's blog post series about boards. "Designing the Ideal Board Meeting Series," *VC Adventure*. https://sethlevine.com/archives/category/designing-the-ideal-board-meeting-series (accessed January 14, 2022).
2. Attorney-client privilege is a legal concept that allows certain communications between a client (in this case, the company) and attorney to be kept confidential and non-discoverable during any legal proceedings.
3. Jeff Bussgang, "Board Meetings vs. Bored Meetings," *Boston VC Blog*, April 5, 2011. http://bostonvcblog.typepad.com/vc/2011/04/board-meetings-vs-bored-meetings.html (accessed January 14, 2022).

Chapter 18

Motions and Votes

While a startup may not need a highly formal board meeting, there are still some formal aspects of the meeting that the board should incorporate and follow. These include

- *Notice*: Provide board members advance notice of the meeting, especially if any votes require shareholder approval.
- *Quorum*: Ensure that you have a quorum of the board. While this is often a majority, there are cases where the number of board members that constitute a quorum is defined in the organizing documents.
- *Agenda*: Distribute the agenda in advance of the meeting.
- *Minutes*: Take minutes of the meeting, including a formal record of any motions, votes, and approvals. Outside counsel or the company's general counsel records the minutes.

Robert's Rules of Order

A parliamentary procedure called Robert's Rules of Order[1] governs board meetings. Authored and published by a brigadier general, Henry Martyn Robert, in 1876, these rules have stayed primarily the same over the years. Ironically, Robert wrote the manual in response to his poor performance in leading a church meeting and resolved to learn about the parliamentary procedure before attending another meeting.

Robert's Rules of Order are rules for conduct at meetings that allow everyone to be heard and make decisions without confusion. This approach is a time-tested method of conducting formal business at board meetings, easily adaptable to the style and needs of the company.

Organizations using Robert's Rules of Order typically have a short formal section at the beginning of the meeting, where the meeting is called to order by the chair, a quorum is confirmed, minutes from the previous meeting are approved, and any specific motions made and votes taken for recurring actions such as stock option grants.

While it might feel archaic to mention this, even if a company doesn't formally follow Robert's Rules of Order, the board meeting structure probably follows them. History persists.

Have Your Lawyer at the Meeting

Your company's outside counsel or your internal general counsel should attend every board meeting, if you have one. In addition to recording the minutes, they can advise the board on any specific issues, remind everyone of the requirements on different voting matters (e.g., can the board approve something or is a shareholder vote required?), and create a situation where the discussion at the board meeting is attorney-client privileged.[2] Even if you have an internal general counsel, we recommend outside counsel attend. They are a key business advisor, and having them in the loop makes them more effective when relevant issues arise.

Most lawyers will offer a low, or even free, rate for attending board meetings, especially for early-stage companies. They'll take responsibility for creating the minutes, recording official motions and votes, and creating a governance platform and appropriate behavior that future investors will value.

The Mechanics of Voting

Board members can present motions or request them to be added to the agenda. These motions are proposals for the entire board to act upon during the meeting. Presenting and approving motions are defined by the bylaws of a company.

Technically, early-stage companies will seldom have much protocol and fanfare, and it's unlikely that your board will follow an elaborate parliamentary procedure. However, formal board meetings should be conducted to approve and record key action items, especially those that affect all shareholders.

You probably have heard or participated in proposals for motions and the ensuing vote. The process has several steps, regardless of formality. Generally, the topic is brought up and discussed. After the discussion, someone makes a motion, after which it's seconded. Then, you (or your lead director) call for a vote. Directors say "Yes" or "No," after which the vote is approved or denied.

In most situations in early-stage companies, these are non-controversial formalities. However, making sure everyone is heard, approves or disapproves of the motion, and the vote is recorded are essential for good governance.

In the world of videoconferencing, getting "yeas" and "nays" recorded can be difficult. Simpler methods allow everyone to give "thumbs up" or "thumbs down." Alternatively, asking "Is anyone opposed?" is a good way to hear any objections.

There are two other relevant motions. The *motion to table* is used in an attempt to kill a motion. The *motion to postpone* is a strategy that gives opponents visibility into the support or lack thereof regarding the motion without calling the motion to a vote. Both are rare in VC-backed companies.

What If You Don't Agree?

Conflict and disagreement can arise between various board members, especially investors and management. Try to address and resolve it outside the context of a board meeting. If that's not possible, make sure there's ample time during the board meeting for a discussion and an effort to resolve the disagreement.

Occasionally, the board will decide something outside the context of a board meeting. This decision is often around financing or change in leadership, especially concerning the CEO. In these situations, while it may feel like there is uniform agreement on a course of action, there may be differing views or changes in perspective as the board members discuss the nuances of the decision. Some board members are dogmatic, feeling that it should be executed regardless of feedback once a decision is made. We've found that continuous, open, and constructive discussion, especially when there's uncertainty or points of difference, is a powerful way to work through the issue at hand.

On early-stage boards, if you get to the point of a serious conflict, make sure you know who will support an issue well in advance of any formal activity. Then, approach the situations where there are disagreements with real formality, following the appropriate procedures. Resolve the issue, make your decisions, and move past the conflict.

Dealing with Formal Items

Given that there will always be some formal activity at any board meeting, address formal items upfront, especially matters requiring votes. This ordering is contrary to the flow of many startup company board meetings, where the CEO uses the meeting to set issues up and then crams in a bunch of formal decisions at the end when everyone is running out of time.

Several years ago, Brad tried turning the agenda upside down at all of his board meetings. The formal stuff went first. Everything else followed. The result was a much more engaged and informed board meeting. If formal items required discussion, they were dealt with at the beginning of the meeting when everyone was fresh and alert. If formal discussions needed more time or more information, that became clear quickly, and were allocated the appropriate amount of time.

While formal items typically don't require a lot of discussions, they occasionally do, and there seems to be a high correlation between having important voting items left and having no time left to talk about them. By addressing the formal issues at the beginning of the meeting and giving everyone enough time to address them, the balance of the meeting is free to follow whatever tangents it wants, without the anxiety building about running out of time to get to the formal items.

Minutes

By law, one needs to create minutes to prove a legally held board meeting and establish the topics the board heard about and discussed. The board minutes show that the board complies with all of its legal duties.

Formally, the secretary records the minutes of any board meeting. Company counsel or outside counsel prepares the minutes, which are part of formal corporate records. Most boards formally approve the minutes from the previous board meeting at each subsequent meeting. Keep all minutes from all board meetings well-labeled in a single online folder. You'll need them whenever you do a corporate transaction.

Some of the topics at the meeting, especially voting issues, should be recorded in detail. For instance, if the board votes to issue options to employees, take on a new round of financing, settle litigation, or sell the company, these actions and the corresponding motions and resolutions should be carefully detailed and accurately recorded.

In contrast, the regular business of a board meeting doesn't need extensive documentation. Many lawyers feel that less detail is better, since the minutes may lead to an unwanted blueprint if a plaintiff's lawyer decides to come after you for some reason. In general, you want the minutes to be detailed enough to show that the board focused on the correct issues but not detailed enough to allow someone to nitpick the meeting later.

Remember that you need a quorum of the board to take an official vote. Usually, a quorum is a majority of the board, and a motion requires a majority of the attendees to pass. If you don't have a quorum present, you don't have an official board meeting and can't take any official actions.

Unanimous Written Consent

Besides taking official votes at board meetings, the board may also act by unanimous written consent. This type of consent involves a document prepared by your lawyers that often contains more detailed information than what the minutes would look like for a particular vote. The only difference is that the board isn't together during a meeting but instead approves the motion asynchronously via signatures to a document. You need unanimous consent to authorize this kind of action.

There are situations where you want to show in the minutes that the board deliberated on a specific item, even if all the directors aren't in attendance. In these situations, convene the meeting (or have the discussion in the existing board meeting), record the attendance and conversation in the minutes, and get formal approval separately via unanimous written consent.

Notes

1. Brad's wife, Amy Batchelor, co-author with Brad of *Startup Life: Surviving and Thriving in a Relationship with an Entrepreneur* (Feld and Batchelor, 2013), loves Robert's Rules of Order. Whenever Brad is getting too unstructured about how he interacts with her, she simply invokes Robert's Rules, which always gets him to focus on what is going on around him.
2. Make sure you understand the rules of when something is attorney-client privileged (ACP) and when it isn't. For example, ACP applies only when company counsel, directors, and employees are in the room. A single board observer in the meeting may break ACP. And the mere presence of a lawyer does not establish ACP. Many people don't understand ACP and refer to it indiscriminately. Skadden has a great top-10 list of misconceptions about ACP: https://www.skadden.com/insights/publications/2021/04/the-informed-board/just-between-you-and-us.

Section 4

Between Meetings: Ongoing Work

Chapter 19

Managing Ongoing Communication

Board members have specific expectations around communication from the CEO. A VC board member will likely serve on multiple boards and sees all kinds of board meetings and communication. In contrast, you may not have similar experiences and often learn to manage board expectations in real time. Ultimately, it's your responsibility to manage expectations around communication to the board.

What the Board Expects from a CEO

You run the show. If you take responsibility for your decisions, your board will respect you, even if your decisions turn out to be wrong. When you and the board agree to certain action items, you ultimately have to live with the consequences of the decisions. Weak CEOs hide behind their board, saying, "The board decided we should do Y." By doing this, you abdicate your responsibility and set up a negative dynamic between the board and your management team.

Good boards don't say, "We want the company to do thing X." Rather, they participate in a discussion about the topic and, with you, reach a consensus. In any robust board discussion, participants may disagree, and you may not know what to do. Ultimately, a good board comes to a decision and moves on.[1] If you disagree with the board on a decision, make sure you present your case well. But once the board decides, it's yours to execute.

The only actual operating decision that a board ever makes is to fire the CEO. Sure, the board and individual board members are often involved in many operational decisions, but the ultimate decisions should be yours. If you aren't in a position to be the ultimate decision-maker, you shouldn't be the CEO. And if board members don't trust you to decide, they should take one of two actions available to them: either leave the board or replace you.

If you have a board constantly telling you what to do, it should be a sign of concern. Greg Sands (Managing Partner, Costanoa Ventures) says, "The CEO lives and breathes this business 80 hours a week. We are screwed if you don't know more than we do." In a situation where a board member is constantly directing you to do something, confront them about it and, if necessary, include your lead director in the discussion. It could be a style issue from an overbearing board member or a critical situation or concern of the board that you don't hear properly. You have a responsibility to be proactive in this situation, figure out what is going on, and address it directly.

Good boards care about growing the business and address critical issues clearly with a regular cadence of communication. They also care about the company's ability to attract customers, recruit and retain team members, and execute its financial plan. But good board members often don't care about trivial things. Tim Miller describes his first board meeting.

> *I was concerned that the board might be worried that my wife was in charge of the money and I was in charge of the company, so I spent 30 minutes going line item by line item on the financials with rigorous detail about things like telephone and rent expenses. The board members said, "Hey, we trust you, and we wouldn't have given you $3.5 million if we thought you were going to steal the money." I had no idea what to expect—I tried to put myself in their shoes and offered this level of detail, which they did not care about.*

Communicate Both Good and Bad News

Daily, some things go right while others go wrong. As CEO, you're endlessly barraged with good and bad news. You and your leadership team talk about and deal with many things that aren't working.

While your board enjoys hearing about victories and successes, they also expect to hear about problems and failures.

When you surface bad news with a plan to address it and then effectively solve the problem or come up with a new approach, you build credibility with the board. Being proactive about challenges and soliciting input from your board involve them in the issue directly, rather than just as bystanders. Ultimately, you'll build enduring trust with your board by being transparent.

The difference in speed and frequency with which good news gets shared versus bad news matters. Consider how your board will react if you send weekly "we are awesome" emails but only bring up a problematic issue two months after it first surfaced. You might have thought you had solved the problem when it first came up, but if it festered or if a board member could have helped you address the issue, it's a missed opportunity. If this pattern repeats, it reduces your credibility.

Surprises at board meetings are a particular problem. If all of the communication between board meetings is about how well things are going, and then the board meeting is full of broken stuff, your credibility with the board declines. The inverse is also true; don't be endlessly negative when things are going well. Find a balance and communicate regularly between board meetings.

How often should you communicate? It depends on the stage of the startup, the context of your current situation, and the preferences of your board. A weekly written update can be helpful at the early stages, given the number of new experiments and things changing. Some CEOs, and some boards, enjoy this rhythm of communication. Others prefer a less frequent cadence unless an urgent issue needs to be addressed. Ideally, discuss a proposed communication cadence with the board and be consistent.

Matt is trying something new at Bolster, cc'ing the board and observers on his weekly Friday email to the entire company. Although not directed at the board, this email gives directors regular reports of good news, bad news, metrics, milestones, and other thoughts Matt wants to share. The feedback he's gotten so far is that this works well to keep the board's finger on the organization's pulse without any added communication overhead.

When you know you have a controversial issue you want to discuss, give it time and space to breathe. Bring it up in a discussion format rather than forcing a decision. Talk about the pros and cons of what you'd like to do. Get feedback. Let some time pass while you collect more data, and then communicate the new information. Balance the positive and negative aspects of the decision, but incorporate your preference.

Finally, make sure you and your board are aligned on how you are communicating. Upside surprises, while pleasant, tend to have a less emotional impact than downside surprises. If your goal is to set expectations low and always overachieve, make sure the board doesn't view this as sandbagging. Or, if you are always coming up just short of your stretch goals, make sure your board understands why you are setting stretch goals and how you are communicating them to your team.

Note

1. Brad covers this in greater detail, see Brad Feld, "Note to CEOs: Decisions Come from You, Not the Board," *Feld Thoughts*, July 11, 2011. http://www.feld.com/wp/archives/2011/07/note-to-ceos-decisions-come-from-you-not-the-board.html (accessed January 14, 2022).

Chapter 20

Committees

Early in a company's life, there are rarely separate board committees. However, as the company, and the board, grow, two committees generally are created: Compensation and Audit. As companies get closer to an initial public offering (IPO), a third committee—Nominating—is created.

Each committee generally has at least two board members on it, with one acting as the committee's chair. Generally, the committees make recommendations to the full board instead of being responsible for the actual decisions. The committee charter, which your outside counsel can easily draft, defines the scope of authority for each committee. Depending on your charter, the CEO will either sit on all committees directly or ex-officio, which means they will attend all committee meetings without actually having a committee vote.

While the committees don't have to meet before the board meeting, having a regular tempo around the committee meetings as your company grows creates formality and ensures regular board-level conversations around compensation and audit issues.

Committee Meeting Formalities

Ideally, each committee meeting is up to an hour and happens the day before or the same day as the board meeting. Then, at the beginning of the board meeting, each committee chair gets a short session of under ten minutes to do a read-out from the committee meeting along with any recommendations for the board to consider.

As with all meetings, each committee meeting should have formal minutes. Your counsel or board secretary should write up the minutes, which should be approved at the beginning of the next committee meeting alongside and then appended to your board meeting minutes.

In addition to the committee members, any board member can attend a committee meeting. Additionally, outside counsel and the company's general counsel, if one exists, should attend. You should attend all committee meetings. Your CFO should attend compensation and audit. Your HR leader should attend compensation and nominating.

As with a board meeting, at the end of the committee meeting, all members of management should leave the meeting so the board members on the committee can have a discussion without management in attendance.

Compensation

The compensation committee is responsible for defining the CEO's compensation and establishing guidelines for executive compensation, including base and bonus pay, along with any equity compensation.

When a company is young, the compensation structure usually is straightforward. But, as companies get bigger, even if there are well-defined guidelines, there end up being lots of exceptions, especially in a competitive hiring environment. The compensation committee is your partner in this process, especially as you are trying to land a key executive who doesn't fit nicely into whatever compensation structure you have established.

Many resources exist to help propose and evaluate executive compensation. The most widely used database is the Venture Capital Executive Compensation Survey (VCECS), which is run every year by Morgan Stanley's Shareworks/Option Impact unit, and is free for participating companies. As your company matures, you'll hire HR and equity consultants to help you benchmark and define future compensation plans. The compensation committee should be deeply involved in all aspects of any process with an outside consultant.

If you have a good compensation committee, the recommendations to the board will be well defined. Occasionally there will be a board discussion around some aspect of the proposals. When this happens, don't rush it, as you want all board members to sign off on anything around compensation. The compensation committee can be chaired by any director.

Audit

The audit committee is responsible for choosing outside auditors and approving the audit fee, usually based on the recommendation of management. While management works with the outside auditors, they report to the audit committee. Most VC-backed companies must get an annual audit, although this has loosened up a lot, especially for early-stage companies, in the past decade. However, if a company raises bank debt of any sort, the lender will almost certainly require an audit.

The audit process is an important check and balance on the company. Most young companies have immature systems with many control issues. The auditors will point these out and it's up to the board to decide how comfortable it is with the controls. As companies get closer to an IPO, all aspects of the audit and control systems become more critical, and the work becomes more serious.

While your company may have a strong CFO and solid financials, the accounting rules constantly change. The audit surfaces inconsistencies with your financials, especially if you are accounting for some aspect of your business that doesn't conform to current accounting standards. While private, a US-based company will be audited under the AICPA standards. When you go public or get acquired by a SPAC, you will be subject to PCAOB standards. You may not know or care about this, which is one of the benefits of having an audit committee that pays attention to it.

The audit committee pays attention to several other topics. Any private stock sales between employees and shareholders, especially any formality around them such as ROFRs (rights of first refusal) and co-sale rights, should be reviewed by the audit committee in advance of any transaction. If the company has a whistleblower policy, the audit committee should review and enforce it. Finally, any complex accounting issues, especially acquisitions, should be presented to the audit committee.

Public companies have to adhere to specific standards for audit committee members around financial literacy. As a result, audit committees typically are filled by people who have been partners in public accounting firms, CFOs, or CEOs. In all cases, you want a very experienced audit committee chair.

Nominating

Most young companies don't have a nominating committee, but this becomes an important committee as an IPO approaches. Often, the nominating committee is referred to as the nominating/governance committee and covers all aspects of how the board governs. Responsibilities include running the selection process for directors, succession planning for the board, committee staffing and responsibilities, performance assessment and compensation of board members, insurance, and overall corporate governance policies and documentation. The nominating committee can be chaired by any director.

CEO Expenses

Although not usually in formal charter of either the compensation or audit committees, an annual review of the CEO's expenses is a good practice for either of those committees, or for the board as a whole. For about a decade at Return Path, no one approved Matt's expenses. Then there was a scandal at a large company that caught Matt's eye about a CEO abusing his expenses and getting fired for it. Consequently, Matt decided it was time to put a formal CEO Expense process in place.

Once a year, you should aggregate all of your expenses for the full year, from everything that goes through a regular expense report to everything that doesn't, including things that are billed to the corporate card. Pull out things that aren't personal, like Pizza Friday for the office or extra fans during a heatwave. Categorize all expense items, analyze them on a per-night, per-trip, or per-person basis as appropriate, footnote extraordinary items, and compare them to the prior year's number for the same line item. The full board, or whichever committee your board decides, reviews them and confirms that everything is in the range of what is reasonable.

Chapter 21

Mentors and Learning by Doing

Some CEOs feel they should never show any weaknesses. One VC remarked that one of their portfolio CEOs once said, "Hey, you need to know this. My father passed away unexpectedly." He shared this news with his board members several days after this event occurred. The CEO may have felt the need not to show any weakness in this case. This board member quickly offered the CEO the following advice: "No one expects you to be a robot, carrying the weight of the world around with no emotion. Things are much easier to deal with when you get them out in the open."

Mentorship and Vulnerability

In another situation, a CEO described dealing with a suicidal employee. "So yesterday, this guy put a gun in his mouth and threatened to kill himself. Two other employees went to his house to talk with him and essentially rescue him from himself. And then today, he showed up to work. What should I do? I can't cry in my chairman's beer."

We disagree. While having deep personal relationships with each of your board members is unlikely, it's helpful to be vulnerable with at least one of your board members. Furthermore, some board members are willing to engage in mentorship-type relationships, where there is an explicit understanding that you will share things with them about what you are personally struggling with to be more effective.

Nicole Glaros (Chief Investment Strategy Officer, Techstars) gives the following advice to board members:

> *If you're a mentor, you should strive to be trusted. I use a simple test as a metric to know how I'm doing. Am I the first phone call a CEO makes when something goes wrong? It's a simple measure of how much trust you have established with the CEO. When the CEO trusts you, they'll approach you with all sorts of problems. Your collective brainpower leads to more constructive and successful outcomes. While establishing trust can be elusive, it starts with the behaviors and orientations of the board member, not the CEO, and most often reveals its true nature during times of crisis. Rather than see a phone call as an annoyance or distraction, I see it as confirmation that the CEO trusts me.*

As you develop trusted relationships with board members, you will open up with them. While the board should not become a substitute for a psychologist, hopefully, you will find a board member who never:

- Says "I told you so . . ."
- Tells you one thing in private and the opposite in the boardroom.
- Tries to be right all the time or show you how smart they are.
- Surprises you or neglects to inform you of something.
- Flatters the lead, or loudest, investor.
- Plays a game like giving the silent treatment or going dark if they disagree with you.

Over time, the best mentorship relationships go both ways, becoming "peer-mentorship" situations where both people learn from each other. This is true of all aspects around vulnerability. While some people draw bright lines between personal and professional relationships, our experience is that a culture of communication, peer-mentorship, friendship, and mutual respect is more effective.

Learning by Doing

The best way to learn about being a board member is to be an outside director for another company. While you may be tempted to look to join a board for a company further along than yours, the company's size doesn't matter (and practically speaking, that may be impossible to find). No startup follows a linear path of progress, and every CEO has fantastic days, dismal days, and lots of in-between days. Being a director of another company will teach you many things that will help you be more effective, including working with your board.

Matt has regularly sat on outside boards while running both Return Path and Bolster and has gleaned valuable insights from those experiences into his leadership style and how to address issues facing his business. He leaves those meetings with a page of notes from the company's board meeting and ideas and topics for his own company that came to him during the meeting.

Following are a few examples of the value of sitting on an outside board:

- **Build a Detached and Objective View of Challenging Situations:** As an outside director, you will learn to be emotionally and functionally detached from the pressure and dynamics of what the company CEO is going through while still understanding the issues. From this, you will get a broader perspective on how the job of a CEO works.
- **Build Empathy for Your Board:** You might have new empathy for a CEO, including self-empathy, since you are also a CEO. This is a difficult concept for some, but fundamentally it is about understanding yourself better, especially when you are in emotional distress or intellectually challenged. You'll empathize with other board members, appreciate your board members more, and discover approaches to developing a more effective relationship with them.
- **Acquire a Deeper Understanding of Board Duties and Responsibilities:** You'll be on the other side of the financing discussions as a board member. You'll understand the concept of fiduciary responsibility more accurately. Seeing

board duties from multiple vantage points will improve your ability to present information to your board while understanding better how they'll receive it.

- **Build a Peer Network:** You'll have a peer relationship with another CEO where you have a vested interest in their success. You'll get exposed to new management styles, experience different conflicts, and observe other pressures. The intellectual challenge provided by this experience will make you a stronger CEO.

One outside board relationship at a time is appropriate. Not two, not three—just one. As an active CEO, you just won't have time to be serious and deliberate about multiple boards. While you might feel like you have the capacity for more, your company needs, and deserves, your attention first. There are exceptions, especially for experienced CEOs or serial entrepreneurs who have a unique relationship with an investor, but one outside board is generally plenty.

Chapter 22

CEO Transitions

As discussed earlier, the board only makes one operational decision—hiring and firing the CEO. While CEO and board conflict can often get resolved, there are points in the startup journey where the board decides it's time for a new CEO. Sometimes this is a surprise to the CEO; other times, it's a graceful transition. Either way, it's one of the most significant and intense things that a board takes on.

Situations That Lead to a CEO Change

Many specific situations lead a board to make a CEO change. Some are cut and dry, like fraud or other illegal behavior on the part of the CEO. But most are subjective and often result in long, difficult deliberations on the part of the board before making a final decision. These situations test the mettle of investors and independent board members and often shape the board's future culture and communication patterns. One of the most common situations is when the growth of the company stalls. From the outside, the business may look like it's doing fine. But the metrics tell a different story. Development milestones are missed, sales slow down significantly, and the company starts losing its leadership position in the market.

When growth slows, the best CEOs deal with it directly. They aren't bashful about addressing the slowdown and enlisting the board to help determine what to do. While the pressure for results may increase, the worst thing a CEO can do is be in denial or hide from the reality of the situation.

Financing challenges are another common situation that leads the board to question whether a CEO has what it takes to continue leading the company. Remember the three things Fred Wilson says a CEO is responsible for: (1) set the overall vision and strategy of the company and communicate it to all stakeholders, (2) recruit, hire, and retain the very best talent for the company, and (3) make sure there is always enough cash in the bank.[1] When raising additional capital stalls, a board will often explore whether the CEO is failing at any of these three things. While not always the case, difficult financings can create stress and generate conflict between the board and the CEO.

A steady exodus of key people is another signal to a board to dig deeper to see if the CEO is up for the job. While turnover, including on the leadership team, is a regular part of the growth and development of any company, if senior people regularly leave voluntarily for jobs at other companies, this can be a strong signal that something is wrong at the top.

Finally, conflict arises when the CEO and the VC board members are at cross-purposes about the company's goals. For example, the CEO wants to sell, and VC board members want to keep growing the business. Or, this can be because the VC board members want to sell, and the CEO wants to keep going. The example of Zappos, which was a successful exit, shows a positive way that this can be resolved.

> We had a tough time convincing our board of directors who were also our investors to embrace many of our activities that would help build the Zappos brand and make the world a better place. The directors didn't fully understand or were not convinced of things like brand or culture, dismissing many of these as "Tony's social experiments." Sequoia expected an exit in five years and hadn't signed up for these additional things. I was pretty close to being fired from the board. I was learning that alignment with shareholders and board of directors was just as important.
>
> Tony Hsieh (Zappos, founder)[2]

Scale Up with Growth

In a survey of 212 companies conducted by Noam Wasserman (a Harvard Business School professor), by the time the ventures were three years old, 50% of the founders were no longer the CEO. By year four, only 40% were still in the corner office, and fewer than 25% had led their company's IPOs. In a separate study, this theme was validated even though some outcomes were different. Professor Steven Kaplan (University of Chicago Graduate School of Business) studied 50 venture-backed companies that evolved from business plan to IPO and found that management turnover is substantial. Founders get eliminated quickly along the way: only 49% of the VC-backed founders stayed till the IPO.[3]

As an entrepreneur, consider your range and how far you can take the startup. Tim Miller says, "The single most important question I got from a board member was 'Can I take this startup to 200 people? To 1000 people?' I took it as a challenge. I grew a lot with the help of my board."

Matt wrote a lot about this topic in *Startup CEO* (Blumberg, 2020). Following is a summary of his thoughts on scaling yourself as a CEO:

- Make it a priority and be intentional about doing it.
- Study the craft of running a larger organization by reading relevant books and articles and asking later-stage CEOs to let you spend time shadowing them, or at least picking their brain.
- Work with a CEO coach.
- Join or start a CEO peer group.
- Hire a great Executive Assistant or Chief of Staff and learn how to leverage them to create more time for yourself.
- Use your board and any advisors as regular sounding boards in 1:1 meetings, not just in full board meetings.
- Make gathering feedback on yourself a priority—a full 360 review once every 12–18 months goes a long way toward learning what you need to work on to scale as a CEO.

Why Boards Fire CEOs

There are a variety of reasons that boards fire CEOs. Some are good and rational, while others are bad and inconsistent. A few common examples follow:

- **The CEO Is a Control Freak:** A CEO was fired because, despite their performance, they were a control freak. "No decisions could be made by anyone. It became unnerving as we looked at the challenges in attracting A players. We finally decided to fire the CEO in the long-term interests of everyone," says the VC, who served on the company's board.
- **The CEO Is Directionally Challenged:** A startup, receiving rave reviews in scientific and business media, established its market direction in diagnostics. As the new CEO came on board, he saw a compelling opportunity in the defense sector and wanted to shift directions. "He almost hijacked the company. Three months into his role, we didn't feel right, and, six months later, we knew for sure this was the wrong guy," says the chair of the board. After burning through millions of dollars, the CEO was fired. The company suffered a down round in its next financing event—it took six years to recover, but it was eventually acquired for over $200 million. The opportunity in diagnostics prevailed even as defense spending dried up.
- **The CEO Doesn't Scale:** As the company grew, the founding CEO was on their third startup but couldn't scale. They were always sitting in their neat corner office and never took the time to understand the product's intricacies. They dropped prices when it was unnecessary, compromising the company's financial future. The manufacturing process required managing vendors and inventory and maintaining productivity. The founding CEO was a creative type but had lost their enthusiasm. "How can a CEO who is making something so exciting sound so dull and boring?" a prospective investor asked a board member. The discipline and operational skills required to scale the company were utterly lacking. "Even though we were doing so well, we didn't see this CEO taking the company to an IPO," said a

VC board member. But it'd take over a year to get the board aligned to replace the CEO.

- **It's Time for Change:** One entrepreneur we interviewed pointed out that they were ousted when the company raised a Series B financing. The new investors believed that replacing a CEO would accelerate the company's growth. The new CEO was brought in, and didn't perform, which led to another CEO change about 18 months later. The company eventually folded. The entrepreneur said, "We had three CEOs in three years. I felt the board wasn't familiar with the market, and we ended up with inaction or conflicts rather than quick decisions. I felt some board members were unfamiliar with the business: they were financial investors who didn't have much startup experience."

- **A Stronger CEO Becomes Available:** A first-time CEO started a life science company and steadily built it for five years, raising multiple venture rounds. However, they were replaced when a highly accomplished candidate (a CEO who had an IPO and two successful prior exits) became available. The founder had no exits as yet. Since the candidate had deep relationships with potential acquirers and had demonstrated the ability to sell companies, the board promptly voted to replace the founder.

- **The CEO Cannot Enter the Building:** A VC we interviewed shared that the CEO of one of their portfolio companies couldn't enter the building due to a pending harassment case initiated by one of the key employees. After the investigation, the board promoted the CFO to acting CEO and terminated the CEO.

While entrepreneurs can be slow to recognize their shortcomings and ask for help, VCs are often too quick to jump the gun and seek a change of guard. Manu Kumar says, "VC behavior reminds me of that song 'If I had a hammer'—unfortunately, most VCs have a hammer, and the nail is the CEO. A company's problems do not necessarily go away by firing the CEO, and at times, that may be the worst of all options." When a startup hits the ceiling (or bottom), some VCs default to hiring a new CEO.

Planning for Healthy Transitions

CEO transitions can occur under a few predictable circumstances, and it's beneficial for both the board and the CEO to formulate a simple outline to conduct this transition with minimal grief and drama. The following are some things that a board should communicate to a CEO in this context:

- **Performance:** Establish annual metrics of CEO performance in conjunction with the board. A CEO should control and impact these metrics and have adequate resources to execute the plan. The CEO knows performance warning signs—the metrics start to falter.
- **Chemistry and Cohesion:** While performance matters, as companies grow, the ability to build a cohesive team of high performers is equally important. The best CEOs attract fantastic people. On the other hand, CEOs who cannot delegate attract mediocre people.
- **Decision-Making Process:** The board should offer warning signs to alert the CEO of lack of performance or team issues. While startups don't have the cash cushion or the luxury of extended periods of performance remediation, the relationship with the board will determine how these are communicated to the CEO.

Once the decision has been made to part ways, the CEO and board should share this appropriately with the team members. Such situations can be highly emotional, and some CEOs, especially founders, can have a negative reaction. The healthy transition often goes awry if this happens, and the CEO is subsequently escorted out of the building. It's in both the board's and the CEO's interest to work together so the situation doesn't deteriorate.

A founder/CEO may shift into a new role in some situations. A classic example is a technical founder/CEO who moves to CTO when a new CEO joins the team. Another case is the CEO, who becomes executive chair, staying engaged with the business in a non-decision-making role. If the transition is smooth and harmonious, such role changes can lead to more substantial outcomes for the company.

Notes

1. Fred Wilson, "What a CEO Does," *AVC*, August 30, 2010, n. 8. http://www.avc.com/a_vc/2010/08/what-a-ceo-does.html (accessed January 7, 2022).
2. Tony Hseih, *Delivering Happiness: A Path to Profits, Passion, and Purpose* (New York: Grand Central Publishing, 2010).
3. Steven N. Kaplan, Berk A. Sensoy, and Per Stromberg, "Should Investors Bet on the Jockey or the Horse? Evidence from the Evolution of Firms from Early Business Plans to Public Companies," *Journal of Finance*, February 2009. https://www.hhs.se/contentassets/662e98040ed14d6c93b1119e5a9796a4/kaplansensoystrombergjf2009.pdf (accessed January 15, 2022).

Section 5

Transactions

Chapter 23

Financings

The dynamics around a financing vary dramatically, but your board always plays a role in the process. While board members, especially VCs, play an active role in raising money, finding new investors, and negotiating terms, they also have an essential governance role.

Every financing has a formality around it. Legal documents must be negotiated, including a stock purchase agreement. The board approves formal resolutions associated with the financing and signs multiple documents.

As with any transaction, it's critical to have an experienced lawyer involved. Your brother-in-law, who specializes in divorce law, isn't the right choice. Make sure you have experience on your team.

We aren't going to go into financings in-depth—for that, read *Venture Deals* (Feld and Mendelson, 2019). However, we'll explore several different situations and the unique responsibilities of the board in each.

New Investor-Led Round

The easiest financing transaction happens when a new investor leads the round. In this case, the board's duties are straightforward. The conflicts are limited because an outsider, who has no prior interests in the company, drives the terms. There will be a long list of resolutions associated with the financing, but these are standard and rarely controversial.

As with any transaction, there's value to formality. Hold a board meeting, take attendance, discuss fiduciary duties, propose motions, and take votes. Then, memorialize the resolutions in the minutes.

Insider-Led Round

There's a potential conflict when an existing investor leads a round, especially if that investor also has a board seat. There are two key issues: (1) whether the pricing is fair to all shareholders, and (2) if the directors have fulfilled their duty of care to the company.

In an insider-led round, it's important that all board members, especially the outside directors, participate in the deliberations. The investor board member leading the round should explicitly acknowledge their conflict, and the non-conflicted board members should freely express their opinions.

Matt led the Return Path board through a series of insider-led rounds. When one of the rounds became contentious, Matt brought a pile of company logo hats to a board meeting with two different colors and said, "Today, most of us are here wearing two hats." He gave everyone on the board a gray hat. He then gave each investor director a blue hat. He asked that the investor directors wear the gray hat when speaking from their perspective as a board member, but then put on the blue hat when they switched to an investor perspective. While a little corny, it was highly effective. The technique cut the tension in the room and forced everyone to recognize that the conversation was rife with conflicts while clarifying each director's perspective.[1]

Ultimately, voting dynamics depend on the rights in the certificate of incorporation, as defined by the voting rights agreement from the earlier financing transaction. If the round happens at a price equal to or greater than previous rounds, the main focus of the discussion should be on whether the financing is fair and if the existing, non-conflicted shareholders support it. While formal approval of all shareholders is unlikely to be required, if there is any concern, do a rights offering.

The Down Round and a Rights Offering

A *down round* occurs if the price of the new round is lower than the previous round. If a new investor leads the down round, the board doesn't have any special responsibilities beyond those in a typical financing. However, if an existing investor leads a down round, the board needs to be sensitive to conflicts.

The best way to address the situation where an existing investor leads a down round is to do a *rights offering* to all shareholders. A rights offering is a legal process that gives every investor a chance to purchase their pro-rata in the financing even if they don't have formal pro-rata rights.

The best way to execute a rights offering is to first close the financing with the existing major investors and then do a rights offering to all shareholders. While this involves extra paperwork and effort, it eliminates the risk that a minority shareholder might complain later that the financing wasn't in the best interest of the company. This situation is one you want an independent board member to bless, which is another reason to have independent board members at all company stages.

How Involved Should VCs Be in Financings?

Some VCs claim to have unique, magic skills that help any company raise future financing rounds. While some VCs are much better at raising money than others, financing the company is the responsibility of the CEO.

A common mistake of first-time CEOs is to expect that once they get a VC on board, they'll have an easier time raising money in the future. An experienced CEO knows that every financing process is unique. Many are challenging due to circumstances exogenous to the company, such as the macroeconomy, the sudden presence of a new competitor, or the activity levels of target VCs.

Convertible Notes

Many financings, especially early-stage or bridge financings, are done using convertible notes or a similar instrument like a SAFE.[2] If the convertible note is structured and proposed by a new investor, the board has the same responsibility as in a new investor-led financing. If an existing investor is making the proposal, the board has the same responsibility as in an insider-led financing. In both cases, the documentation is different, but the responsibilities are the same.

In some cases, the convertible note will be a bridge loan made by insiders to the next financing. These bridge loans tend to have additional downside protection, including multiples on a sale of the company. Once again, it's important to have independent directors involved, just like in the down round case, so that non-interested parties on the board support the proposal.

Venture Debt

Unlike a traditional loan, which rarely is available for a money-losing VC-backed company, venture debt relies on a company's access to venture capital as the *primary source of repayment* for the loan. Instead of focusing on historical cash flow or working capital assets, venture debt focuses on the borrower's ability to raise additional equity to fund the company's growth and repay the debt.

Experienced lenders have established relationships with VC firms that reduce the likelihood of surprises or misunderstandings. As a result, your VC board members are now the primary source of support for venture debt. Many will care about their reputation with venture debt lenders, so once again, a conflict arises that has a corresponding benefit. You're likely to access venture debt on attractive terms because of your VCs' support. However, if you run into trouble or lose your VCs' support for some reason, you should expect them to be direct and transparent with the venture lender about the situation.

If you borrow venture debt, it's likely to be at the top of the capital structure, above all equity (both preferred and common), and any unsecured creditors. Consequently, the board must pay close attention to the cash level in the company, especially if it enters the zone of insolvency, the point at which a company may be unable to satisfy its obligations to creditors as they come due. When a company reaches the point of insolvency, creditors—including unsecured creditors—join shareholders as parties to whom the board owes fiduciary duties.

For more on venture debt, see Chapter 11 of *Venture Deals*.[3]

Notes

1. For a deeper study of this technique, see Edward de Bono's *Six Thinking Hats* (Boston: Little Brown, 1985).
2. Y Combinator, https://www.ycombinator.com/documents/ (accessed January 14, 2022).
3. Is the chapter title ironic? You decide.

Chapter 24

Stock Option Grants and 409A Valuations

Your board approves all stock option grants. The value of stock options is determined at different points in time. When you grant stock options to employees, the option grant includes the number of shares, the vesting period, and the exercise price. A crucial part of determining the exercise price is coming up with the "fair market value" or FMV of the common stock underlying the option.

Based on Section 409A of the US Internal Revenue Code (referred to simply as "409A"), there are three ways a company can determine the FMV of its common stock.

1. *Board approval:* The company board determines the FMV. If an option holder gets audited and the IRS thinks the strike price isn't the FMV but was artificially low, the option holder has the burden of proof to show otherwise. In this situation, the option holder asks for justification of the FMV from the company. While this used to be standard practice, after 409A rules were modified, this approach is generally no longer used.

2. *Internal expert:* A person internal to the company who has "significant knowledge and experience or training in performing similar valuations" can create a written valuation report detailing the FMV of the common stock. If an inquiry from the IRS occurs, that person's knowledge,

experience, and training could all come under question. Thus, this internal expert option has challenges.

3. *Outside consultant:* The company hires an independent, qualified, experienced valuation firm to create a written valuation report. Voilà! The IRS and the accounting profession just helped create a new cottage industry. When you use this option, the IRS has the burden of proof to show that the valuation was "grossly unreasonable," an almost impossible standard to meet. As a result, this is the best and most common approach used.

Assuming you are using an outside consultant to do the 409A valuation, this consultant will gather financial and financing information. They prepare a lengthy report using numerous valuation methodologies, and conclude with a fair market value for the common stock. The valuation considers several data points, including:

- **The Company:** Assets, debts, capital structure, preferred stock characteristics (its dividends, anti-dilution, liquidation preferences), warrant coverage, and common stock holdings.
- **Its Performance:** Net present value of future cash flows or discounted cash flow and liquidity horizon.
- **The Market:** Comparable transactions along with discounts for lack of liquidity.

Valuation consultants use industry-standard guidelines such as the American Institute of Certified Public Accountants (AICPA) guidelines. These guidelines minimize the voodoo elements of valuation and follow a set of well-defined formulas.

When evaluating an independent valuation firm, consider the following questions:

- **Experience:** How many valuation engagements have been conducted in the past 12 months? 36 months? Have these engagements been in the relevant stage and sector of your startup?

- **Industry Knowledge and Breadth:** How many years of experience do the professionals have in relevant sectors? Does the firm have many professionals in its valuation department?
- **Competency:** Has the firm's valuation methodology been developed using a comprehensive set of data points? Is the report generated using software models or does it blend art and science, including market trends, expertise, and authoritative knowledge of the relevant data points?
- **Quality:** Have any of their valuations been determined "grossly unreasonable" by the IRS? By company auditors? Have they redone any valuations due to errors? Who bears financial liability if their numbers don't hold up and prolong the audit process? Has the firm been directly or indirectly involved in any IRS penalties?
- **Costs:** Are the prices comparable to the market?
- **Speed:** How long does it take to do the analysis?

As with any professional service provider, speak with several clients for references. Also, check with other CEOs, especially those in similar stage companies, to see whom they recommend. Finally, if you have a VC investor, they'll likely have a favorite 409A valuation firm.

Before presenting the 409A analysis to the board, you must be involved in the process. Along with your CFO or VP of Finance, go over the analysis in detail with the 409A valuation firm. It's easy for valuation firms to miss critical data. For example, suppose the valuation firm forgets to consider the preferred stock's liquidation preferences when considering common stock payouts. In that case, the FMV could be off by as much as 75%.

You need to do a new 409A valuation at least once a year. If you have a financing or other corporate event that impacts the company's capitalization or fundamental value, such as acquiring another company, you should do a new 409A analysis immediately.

Chapter 25

Selling a Company

When another company approaches you about buying your company, an intense series of events begins, many of which include your board. The same is true when you and your board decide to sell your company proactively.

Confidentiality

At the beginning of any merger and acquisition (M&A) transaction, both parties (buyer and seller) will enter into a *confidentiality agreement*. A lightweight *non-disclosure agreement* is satisfactory, but your counsel will often recommend additional provisions. The agreements apply to board members, so inform them of what's been signed they can respect them.

A signed term sheet will often include a *no-shop agreement*. This is an agreement by the seller not to engage in any conversation about selling the company with any other party during a specific period, usually between 30 to 60 days. Inevitably, when rumors or leaks occur, outside parties such as the press, investment bankers, or other potential buyers reach out to board members. Given the presence of confidentiality agreements, especially with a non-shop in place, board members should be particularly sensitive to these situations.

Whenever a confidentiality agreement or no-shop agreement is signed, the board should have a deliberate conversion about the presence of the agreement and how each board member should react if contacted by someone regarding the transaction while it is in process.

Finally, board members should be conscientious in situations where the buyer or seller is a public company, as disclosing *material nonpublic information* can lead to insider trading, which is a criminal offense.

Many situations occur that may trip your confidentiality or no-shop agreement. The most likely one is when you receive an unsolicited offer for your company after you have already signed a term sheet to be acquired. Your next call should be to your lawyer for advice when this happens.

Fiduciary Responsibility

The board has a fiduciary responsibility to all shareholders. While easy to say, it's often hard for board members who are also VCs to separate their two roles, especially in an acquisition scenario that provides different consideration for different classes of investors.

The board member has a fiduciary duty to the company. We've discussed this extensively earlier in this book. At the same time, a VC has a fiduciary duty to its LPs. Often, these fiduciary duties are aligned, but they conflict with each other in some cases.

The VC board members should respect their fiduciary duty to the company. If for some reason they can't, they should either resign or should recuse themselves from the board. This should be handled thoughtfully so as not to be disruptive to the transaction. We've been involved in graceful situations where a VC stepped off the board during the transaction so they could vote as a shareholder. We've experienced others where a VC board member shouted, "I'm done with this—I resign from the board," slammed down the phone, and refused to talk to any of the board members directly from that point forward.

It's easy for emotions to take over in these situations. If you see any of your board members tangled up in their conflicts, enlist your lead director, outside counsel, or an outside director experienced with deals, to help navigate the situation. Always try to de-escalate the conflict, as you'll usually need the support of the VC investors to get the deal closed.

Your Outside Counsel's Role

Your outside counsel plays a significant role in selling the company. In addition to handling the paperwork, a great outside counsel is deeply involved in the transaction, helping negotiate the specific terms with the buyer. They're also a calm communicator, helping resolve internal conflicts as they arise, explaining complicated situations clearly, and driving to resolution on ambiguous or contentious situations.

Alessandra Simons (Partner and Co-Chair, Technology M&A at Goodwin Law) has the following thoughts on the role of a lawyer in the sales process.

When it comes to selling a company, founders can make several mistakes that will hurt them, like not involving their M&A lawyer early enough or focusing on price over other items in the term sheet. M&A lawyers, bankers, and VC board members sell companies every day, all day, year after year, and there's a lot of experience to be pulled from them. Bring in your M&A lawyer, not when you get a term sheet, not when the board is thinking about selling, but six months before so they can help package up the company. There will be a laundry list of things from the past where the company lawyer said, "Hey, we should probably do X, or let's think about Y, or the rules have changed for Z." Understandably, a lot of startup companies respond, "We hear you, but it's too expensive, it's going to take too long, we're prioritizing something else." The worst thing you can do is to not fix these items and then hear from a buyer who says, "Wait, you didn't do this? That's $10 million off the purchase price, that's $20 million in an escrow." Cleaning house doesn't have to be expensive and "doing it" can absolutely be done in-house or with outside general counsel.

My one biggest piece of advice: your biggest moment of leverage is before you sign the term sheet, because as soon as you sign the term sheet, it's all downhill from there. There's no version of the universe where, after you sign the term sheet and have agreed on a price, the buyer says, "Oh, my gosh, Aly, this is just a fantastic company that's so much better than you said it was. We're going to give you an extra $10 million." That's just not going to happen. Instead, there are several "price adjustments" to watch out for.

- *Price Certainty*: Cash, debt, and transaction fees will change the price.
- *Closing Certainty*: Are there financial contingencies, or employee issues that have to be solved? Are there thresholds that have to be met before the company is sold?
- *Something Wrong Discovered After Closing*: How much can the buyer reach back into the purchase price and take money back from the stockholders?

(Continued)

(Continued)

This is just scratching the surface of the complexity in selling a company, but bringing in an M&A lawyer and investment banker, leveraging your board, and paying attention to adjustments will help set you up for the best possible outcome.

Alessandra Simons, Partner, Goodwin Law

Your lawyer—or a combination of outside counsel and your general counsel—will work on three things. First is the deal documentation: running the documents, markups, and conducting a good percentage of your negotiations on legal points. Next is working on legal due diligence and producing extensive disclosure schedules. Finally, they'll advise you and your board on key fiduciary responsibilities, shareholder-related laws, and process issues. Even though you and the board make the final decisions, pay close attention to your lawyers.

Acquihire

In recent years, the concept of an *acquihire* has become popular. In this situation, a buyer acquires a company primarily for its employees. As a result, the buyer's motivation is to hire the existing founders and employees rather than value the overall company. Acquihires are popular in downside cases to sell a company "for something" to get a graceful exit.

While the phrase is a trendy one, these transactions are no different from any other company sale. The board has the same responsibilities that it has in any M&A situation. While a buyer will likely focus on getting as much consideration as possible allocated to employees for retention purposes, the board still has to be deliberate about doing the best thing for all shareholders.

Carve-Outs and 280G

Some acquisitions result in all shareholders making a lot of money, while others are less successful. In some cases, companies are sold for less than their liquidation preferences, resulting in all of the consideration in the transaction going to preferred investors and none going to common shareholders and option holders.

Existing management and employees often get nothing in these downside cases unless a specific amount of the consideration is "carved out" by the board. This carve-out has to be agreed to by preferred shareholders, since it is coming out of their consideration. Although you'll often see something between 5% and 20% of the total consideration, there's no standard carve-out amount. Furthermore, the carve-out is almost always allocated only to management and employees currently employed by the company and is often structured to retain them over the next several years after the transaction closes.

A carve-out is considered a *parachute payment* and is covered by Section 280G of the Internal Revenue Code. As a result, there's a formal process as part of any carve-out to do a "280G election" to get an exemption from the parachute tax payments. In this situation, 75% of shareholders not impacted by the carve-out must approve the carve-out to get the exemption from 280G. We suggest you start this process earlier rather than later as we've seen many deals delayed in getting 280G approvals.

Shareholder Representative

There's still work to do after the deal closes and the money trades hands. Someone has to manage the escrow and contend with earn-outs, working capital adjustments, and any litigation concerning reps and warranties that can last long into the future. In every acquisition, the person designated to represent all former shareholders to deal with these issues is called the shareholder representative.

Traditionally, either an executive from the seller or one of the VC board members takes on this role, or you could have a couple of people do it as a committee. If nothing ever comes up, it's a complete non-event for this person. However, when something goes awry where the buyer makes a claim on the escrow or threatens to sue the company's former shareholders, this job becomes a lot of work. The shareholder rep, who typically has a full-time job, little money from the deal (often tied up in escrow) to hire professionals to help, and often isn't a subject matter expert in the issues that arise, ends up being responsible for dealing with it.

Today, a more common approach is to hire a firm that specializes in providing shareholder representation services.[1] The cost of using a firm as a shareholder rep, relative to the deal's overall value, is modest, and you get professionals who spend 100% of their time playing the role of shareholder rep. When there's litigation, they get sued and deal with all the details. Given the wide range of deals they've worked on as shareholder reps, they tend to have wide-ranging and extensive experience with both buyers and their lawyers.

The role of a shareholder representative is discussed in detail in *Venture Deals* (Feld and Mendelson, 2019).

Note

1. One of the first and most established is SRS Acquiom, co-founded by Jason Mendelson. See https://www.srsacquiom.com/ (accessed January 14, 2022).

Chapter 26

Buying a Company

As with the sale of a company, the board will be involved in making acquisitions. However, the board's role in acquisitions is more advisory and less operational than during a sale process.

While the idea of pursuing an acquisition often comes from the management team, it can also come from a board member, since they may know companies to acquire that can grow and strengthen your competitive and economic position. If you're a first-time CEO and have never acquired another company, rely on help from your board throughout the process. Many of your directors will be far more experienced at thinking through and executing a transaction.

Negotiating and Structuring the Deal

There are some circumstances where leveraging one or more of your directors to help with the high-level elements will make sense. In particular, if you are interested in exploring a competitive consolidation, that conversation may be sensitive and hard to broach. Use a director to approach the target, especially if one of your VCs knows the CEO or a director for the company. When Matt's previous company, Return Path, was interested in merging with its top competitor, Veripost, Matt relied on his lead investor, Fred Wilson, to open up the conversation with Brad, Veripost's lead investor. Although Matt and Veripost's CEO, Eric Kirby, ran most operational aspects of the deal, a parallel communication channel between Fred and Brad was essential to negotiating the high-level terms, closing the deal, and the merger's success.

Beyond the initial approach, your board can help structure the transaction. Engaging one or more directors early around this topic will ensure you're optimizing the legal and financial aspects of the transaction while gaining buy-in from directors along the way.

You'll encounter two principal deal structures: an asset purchase and a merger. The buyer often prefers an asset purchase as it is dramatically simpler, carries less risk, and makes it easier to limit liabilities post-transaction. If you're only buying a part of a company, such as a business line or some IP, it's your only choice. If you're buying an entire company, this structure will be less desirable for the seller, who will be left with some liabilities and a shell of a company to wind down after the transaction closes. The seller will prefer a merger, where you purchase the entire company and inherit all of its assets and liabilities. In either case, get feedback from your board upfront around this structural decision.

Financing an Acquisition

You can pay for an acquisition with stock or cash. You can provide additional consideration beyond the upfront deal with an earn-out. Your board can help you think about the tradeoffs, how to combine them, what's feasible for your company at this stage, and what is most likely to work for the seller.

If the acquirer is a private company, an option is to pay with private company stock. This approach is the most difficult to get done because the seller has to trade their illiquid security where they have control for your illiquid security, where they don't have control. One option to make a mostly stock deal more palatable for the seller is to offer a mix of common and preferred stock.

The amount of cash you offer is a function of how much you have on your balance sheet relative to your cash burn and the size of the deal. If cash is a requirement for the seller, consider completing a financing concurrently with (or immediately before) the acquisition. This requires significant buy-in and involvement from your existing investors. Still, many VCs have deep experience using acquisitions to grow companies and will be enthusiastic about providing financing for these opportunities.

Fixed shares and fixed dollar amounts are indisputable. Once the deal is signed, there's nothing more to discuss. Earn-outs for future performance are messier, but they can bridge the "bid/ask" gap in a negotiation. Done well, they mean that you pay more for the deal, but only if it's working out. Done poorly, they can lead to bad feelings or legal battles after the deal. Trust plays a huge role in whatever mechanism you put in place, including trust between your VCs/board and the seller's VCs/board.

For all-cash deals, you will never need to offer a seat on your board or board observer rights, although you may find that the company you're acquiring has an independent director you like and want to retain on your board. For large enough stock deals, you can, or may have to, offer some observer rights or one or more full seats on your board.

Board Approvals

Inform your board of what is happening every step along the way, even for small acquisitions. Your general counsel can outline the specific formal approvals you will need. Table 26.1 is an outline of important checkpoints and whether they are formal or informal.

Table 26.1   Board approvals for an acquisition of another company

Action	Approval type: formal/informal
Thinking about an acquisition	Informal (no approval required)
Approaching a target	Informal
Pursuing a specific target	Formal
Structuring a deal	Informal
Signing term sheet	Formal
Minor changes	Informal
Major changes	Informal/formal (check with counsel)
Close deal	Formal

Managing Transaction and Post-Deal Integration

While this process is generally left to the management team, there are some areas where the board will want to be involved, depending on the size and complexity of the deal. In a low-cost acquihire, IP deal, or tuck-in, you may never hear from your board again beyond questions about how things are going. In a large or "bet the company" competitive consolidation where you add some of your competitor's directors to your board, you may have a special board committee that oversees the integration process and requires regular, dedicated reporting outside board meetings. Be proactive about post-deal integration in all cases, and expect a higher level of accountability and granularity of reporting to your board around any kind of buy-side transaction.

Chapter 27

Going Public

If your company is a huge success and the market allows it, you may be able to take your company public in an initial public offering (IPO). As you march toward an IPO, board responsibilities take on another level of formality. The level of work increases, the presence of lawyers playing an active role is noticeable, and committee work shifts from informal to formal.

While this is an exciting time for a company, the transition from a private company to a public one is serious. As you gear up to go public, there are some specific things that directors should do, and pay attention to.

Process

The process of going public is complex and can take up to a year. In the United States, the Securities and Exchange Commission (SEC) governs this process. Most major law firms have a group dedicated to helping companies through an IPO process.

There are books about the details of the process (many law firms have written books, or at least long marketing documents, about the IPO process). However, the rules are constantly changing. As an entrepreneur, you're fortunate to have lawyers, accountants, and investment bankers who make a living helping companies go public. Use them.

Committees

For private companies, especially early on, the entire board often takes on the functions of individual committees. However, as the company and the board get larger and more mature, creating a formal committee structure makes sense.

As you begin the process of becoming a public company, you should have at least three committees—compensation, audit, and nominating. Each committee should have a formal charter with its responsibilities spelled out. Also, each committee should have at least three independent, non-management board members on it. Some of your VCs will qualify as independent directors, depending on the independence rules, while others won't. One of these independent members should be the committee's chair and be responsible for coordinating all of the committee's activities.

Confidentiality

As with a sale of a company, confidentiality matters around an IPO. However, in addition to typical confidentiality dynamics, IPOs have a special type of confidentiality called a "quiet period." This period begins when the company files its first draft of its registration statement and ends when the SEC declares the registration effective. However, there are many nuances and vagaries around the timing, including a more conservative view by many lawyers that the process should start at the first "organization" (or "org") meeting. Furthermore, in 2005, the SEC relaxed the quiet period rules in some situations.

In the United States, the JOBS Act of 2012 introduced a concept called a "confidential filing." In this situation, companies can now file their draft registration statement confidentially and have it remain so until as few as 15 days before the company commences a roadshow to sell its securities to the public.

In any of these situations, the board needs to be involved in the process and aware of the dynamics around confidentiality. A violation of any of this can jeopardize the entire IPO process.

Insider Status

After a company goes public, board members will be deemed *insiders*. They'll be subject to the same confidentiality and stock trading rules as any other executives in the company. As insiders, they have an exceptionally high standard of confidentiality and duty of care.

VCs on Public Company Boards

Some VCs like to serve on public company boards. Others don't. There isn't an industry-wide best practice, and each VC firm will have its own rules and desires. Make sure you know what your VC thinks about public company board participation well before going public to avoid being surprised.

VCs stay on public company boards for the following reasons:

- The VC simply enjoys being on the board, and public company status doesn't change that dynamic.
- The VC enjoys the "prestige" of being on a public company's board.
- The VC believes that they'll continue to expand their own experience and knowledge base by being on the board post-IPO.
- Company management persuaded the VC to stay on the board.

VCs leave boards before an IPO for the following reasons:

- The VC isn't an expert at dealing with public company compliance issues.
- The VC doesn't want the fiduciary duties of a public company board member.
- The VC doesn't want to be restricted from distributing or selling stock that it holds of the company, which is much harder to do when they are a board member and have insider information.

- The VC is worried about the amount of litigation present for the average public company and doesn't want to be involved in lawsuits.
- The VC is in the business of investing and managing early-stage companies, and the VC's investors don't want them on a late-stage, public board.

SPACs

While SPACs (Special Purpose Acquisition Companies) have been around for decades, they have recently emerged as an alternate way for high-growth companies to go public. Technically, a SPAC is already a public company that acquires a private company. However, through the "deSPAC" process, the private company becomes the surviving entity, effectively "going public."

While the outcome is similar to an IPO, a SPAC is effectively a public company acquiring a private company, so the process is different. Consequently, board dynamics and activities around this type of transaction are more extensive than those in a typical public company acquisition of a private company.

There are two distinct phases with a SPAC transaction: (1) raising a PIPE (Private Investment in Public Equity); and (2) executing the deSPAC transaction. Most SPAC transactions include a PIPE where the joint leadership team of the SPAC and the private company being acquired raise private financing in conjunction with signing the definitive agreement for the acquisition. The PIPE is a critical step in the process, and many SPAC transactions don't get to the definitive agreement because the team is unable to raise the PIPE. During this period, boards have a particularly active role on both sides of the transaction since the PIPE often is the actual valuation mechanism for the transaction. Consequently, boards on each side often have to consider whether to continue with the transaction at different prices.

Assuming the PIPE is raised, the definitive transaction for both the merger and the PIPE will be signed, but no money will flow until the transaction closes. Next, the transaction goes through the deSPAC process. While typical public acquisitions of private companies often have an extended closing process that can include regulatory filings such as Hart-Scott-Rodino (also known as HSR), the deSPAC process is an entirely different beast that consists of multiple SEC filings. At the end of the deSPAC process are two shareholder votes. The first is the redemption vote and is an option for public company shareholders to either keep their shares in the merged company or redeem their shares for cash. The second vote is on the actual transaction.

Assuming the transaction closes, usually, the private company board members become the primary directors of the deSPACed public company, with the SPAC contributing one or two board members. This is the opposite of a typical public company acquisition of a private company and an IPO, where public company shareholders generally remain in place.

Chapter 28

Going Out of Business

Unfortunately, many companies aren't successful, entering bankruptcy or a wind-down process. This situation is one of the most difficult ones for a board to navigate. While cash is certainly tight at this point, investing some of the remaining cash in strong outside counsel and following their guidance is a wise long-term move. If you don't, in addition to the company generating additional liabilities, directors may end up being personally liable for mistakes you and the board make.

Earlier in this book, we discussed the fiduciary duties a board and the board members have to the company and the shareholders. We've also discussed how some board members will have additional duties to others, such as a VC having duties to the limited partners of their fund. When a company begins to fail, the board's fiduciary duties can change. State law defines these duties and differs from state to state. We'll try to give you a general idea of how this works. But, as with everything else in this section, please don't rely on this book for legal advice. Make sure you have a great lawyer.

The Zone of Insolvency

A *solvent* company has the cash to pay its liabilities and financial obligations. If you got your MBA from an esteemed university or were a finance major, you'll start thinking about cash flow versus balance sheet solvency, but for this book, let's keep it simple and say, "If you can pay all your bills, you are solvent."

When a company begins running low on cash, the board must determine if the company is in the *zone of insolvency*. From a legal perspective, the zone of insolvency includes three tests:

- Liabilities exceed Assets on the Balance Sheet.
- There isn't enough cash available to pay the bills.
- The total amount of cash is unreasonably low.

These tests depend on interpretation and cannot be viewed in isolation. At most startups, it's normal to have small amounts of cash in the bank, especially before raising a round of financing.

While in the zone of insolvency, some jurisdictions impose additional duties and liabilities on the board of directors. Failure to recognize this and adhere to the additional duties can lead to personal liability for board members, depending upon state law.

When a company is either in or getting close to the zone of insolvency, the board must meet regularly, which can be as often as multiple times a week, especially if there are potential transactions in play. Each of these should be a formal board meeting with recorded minutes.

Responsibility to Creditors

Normally, boards don't owe a fiduciary duty to creditors. Don't think of creditors as just banks loaning money, but any company liability, including payroll, taxes, rent, catering, Internet service provider, and the copier lease.

Fiduciary duties change once the company enters into the zone of insolvency. At this point, some states impose a fiduciary duty on directors for all "stakeholders," not just shareholders. The board now owes fiduciary duties to any party with a financial interest in the company, which includes all creditors and employees.

Practically, this means that the board must consider all stakeholders' interests when making business decisions. Should the company spend some money to continue building version two of the product, or should they pay off their creditors? Should the company hire a new engineer who could help lead to a new customer sale, or should they pay off their copier lease?

What normally ends up happening is that if the board believes that the value to the company increases by investing in the business, then the company will continue to hire, spend on R&D, or invest in sales. These decisions should be memorialized in the minutes of the meetings. If the board isn't sure, the company should do its best to preserve assets to pay off creditors.

Responsibility to Shareholders

Technically, the board's duties don't change concerning shareholders during these difficult times. If the company is severely underwater, the value of the equity may be zero, which means the board is working to pay off the company's creditors. When in the zone of insolvency, creditors take priority over shareholders.

How the board treats employees is important. For instance, if there is an acquihire situation whereby the creditors are made whole, and the employees find good jobs at the expense of the shareholders receiving nothing, is the board allowed to approve such a deal? Should the board push back to get a return for shareholders by carving out some proceeds from creditors or employees?

Sticky situations can also arise when insider VCs offer a bridge loan to the company, which leads to insolvency instead of a bridge to the next financing. The board, the noteholders (or creditors), and the equity holders can overlap in this situation. Having at least one outside director in the mix is important as it provides an independent voice to support specific transactions.

VCs should know how risky their investing is. For a VC, getting pennies back on dollars invested in a single company doesn't materially impact returns for their fund. Generally, reputable VCs will prioritize creditors and employees above their self-interests in this situation. Because of that, the VC board member will generally also support an outcome that pays off creditors and creates a good situation for employees, at the expense of the shareholders (including them) receiving proceeds.

Finally, the role of banks in lending venture debt is important to consider. Most VCs like to have good relationships with banks to finance their companies. Since the VC is playing for the long term across multiple companies, they'll be particularly focused on trying to get the bank paid back to preserve the VC-bank relationship for future deals.

Liability

Normally, board members don't risk personal liability as long as they follow their fiduciary duties. This is generally the case even in a wind-down situation, but there are exceptions.

Once again, make sure you have a good lawyer by your side. State law determines personal liability issues, which change more frequently than federal law. Depending on where your company incorporates and operates, you may need to follow the laws of both states, which aren't always in alignment. Furthermore, if you aren't in the US or have foreign operations, this gets even more complicated.

When mishandled, a wind-down can result in individual board members being liable for paying wages not paid to employees, for laying off too many people at a particular time, or from creditors who could convince a jury that they should have been paid before the board decided to give severance to employees about to be laid off. We've even seen situations where employees were liable for money received that creditors claimed should have gone to them instead.

If board members resign or approve "fraudulent transfers" (for example, paying shareholders dividends) under such circumstances, they're liable for breaching their duties to the corporation.

Chapter 11

If things cannot be turned around and there's no soft landing sale, then some form of bankruptcy for your company is likely to happen. Bankruptcies can be elected by the board of directors, or in some cases, imposed upon you by nervous creditors who want the company's assets protected by the court.

A Chapter 11 bankruptcy isn't a "going out of business" bankruptcy. Rather, these are reorganizational bankruptcies that normally pay off creditors less than what they are owed while allowing the company to continue operating. When you hear about a large airline or car company "going bankrupt," a Chapter 11 reorganization is usually occurring. You can still buy a car or fly on a plane. During bankruptcy, the company is putting in place and executing a plan to restructure its balance sheet, extinguish large parts of its debt, and continue to operate.

These bankruptcies are rare in the startup world, although they happen with more substantial startups with a lot of debt in their capital structure.

Chapter 7

Chapter 7 bankruptcies, on the other hand, are the "going out of business" type. In this situation, the company's assets are liquidated under court supervision. The company dissolves and ceases to exist. A board vote initiates a Chapter 7 bankruptcy. In some cases, creditors force it upon the company.

This type of bankruptcy is expensive, takes a lot of time, makes more money for the lawyers than the creditors, and is a stain on a board member's resume. If you are later part of a public offering, you'll have to disclose that you were on the board of a company that went bankrupt. If your company isn't massively messed up, you should be able to avoid a Chapter 7 bankruptcy with an *Assignment for the Benefit of Creditors* (ABC).

Assignment for the Benefit of Creditors

This type of wind-down, commonly called an *ABC*, is almost always preferable to a Chapter 7 or Chapter 11 bankruptcy. It's faster and cheaper. It benefits creditors, employees, and shareholders more than lawyers, and it doesn't become part of your resume. Also, it's nearly as safe from a liability standpoint if you choose a qualified company to guide you through the process.

An ABC is a process where the company assigns all the assets and liabilities to a third-party service provider who deals with creditors, sells off assets, and winds down the company. At the assignment, all board members cease to be board members and have no further fiduciary duty liabilities. Going forward, the service provider takes over all management and board-level duties. In short, if they screw up during the wind-down period, it's their problem, not yours.

Generally, good ABC service providers ensure the employees are taken care of to the best of their ability. The service provider sells the remaining assets (everything from office chairs to intellectual property), distributes the cash to the creditors in priority order, and winds down the legal entity.

We've used this process many times and prefer this route both as board members and investors.

Section 6

For Independent Directors and Aspiring Board Members

Chapter 29

Preparing for Your First Board Role

While there are many reasons to join a board, several stand out. These include influencing the company's direction, forging new professional relationships, and learning from the experience. However, board seats, especially for first-time board members, are often challenging to get. How do you land a board role if you have never been a board member? How do you prepare for your first board? More importantly, how can you be a great board member and positively impact the company?

Getting a board position can seem daunting, clubby, and impossible. However, there are plenty of ways to go about this. Many organizations, including Matt's company, Bolster, help with the process, both for board members and companies looking for board members.

To be considered for a board seat, even for an early-stage start-up, you need to bring something to the board that isn't already there. You should have enough operational experience and be senior enough in your company to have functional or industry expertise that's additive to the board. You don't need CEO experience; we've each served on boards with excellent board members who were senior product managers or VPs.

Following are several ways to gain and highlight experience to prepare you to become an attractive candidate for a board position.

- **Board Interactions:** Highlight your historical board interactions. Even if you haven't been a CEO, if you have participated in board meetings, discuss them. Most senior executives in companies with boards will, at some point, have interaction with their board and be called into a portion of (or even most of) every board meeting. CFOs will be reviewing financials with their company's directors. CROs will be on the firing line to explain a soft quarter. Even in brief encounters, this is valuable board experience, and you've likely learned a lot about how a board operates, especially if you've had this experience in multiple companies.

- **Advisory Board:** Another way to prepare for board service is to serve on a formal advisory board. These roles are more common and are found in all sorts of organizations. Although advisory boards aren't as prestigious as corporate boards and don't have formal or legal responsibilities, the issues they face can be every bit as complex, with large budgets, significant assets, and influential stakeholders.

- **Informal Advisory Role:** Many companies have "informal advisory roles," and organizations like Techstars match mentors with very early-stage startups all the time. While the "informal" and "advisory" nature of these roles implies that the position might be more figurehead than substantive, that's not always the case. Highlight the context, the scope, and the actions in which you've been involved.

- **Non-profit Boards:** A board role at a 501c3 non-profit corporation can be just as significant as a for-profit board role. Non-profits range from local to global in the population served, with budgets ranging from hundreds of thousands to hundreds of millions of dollars. In many non-profits, the board is more formalized than in startups, and a non-profit board member may have more substantive committee responsibility than a for-profit board member.

- **Community Organizations:** Board roles and leadership positions in community organizations, including your local Little League team, local Girl Scout chapter, religious organization, or a local city board role, are valuable experiences. Community involvement says a lot about your commitment, values, and willingness to engage with organizations you care about. Like early-stage boards, these boards are often working boards where the volunteers are responsible for governance and oversight and engage in helping the organization's leaders in specific functional areas. Sometimes they go even further and involve doing the actual work, which is a good experience but may not necessarily be a relevant component of corporate board readiness.

- **Training:** There are opportunities to learn corporate governance, board structure, roles, and responsibilities without holding a board seat. Many universities, such as Northwestern, Stanford, Harvard, Wharton, and Santa Clara, offer courses and seminars through their executive education programs. Specific programs such as ACE[1] and Him for Her provide specific training and peer learning opportunities.

Not all CEOs will weigh each of these experiences the same. How you present your experience matters. Unlike a typical resume with a list of bulleted points, a board-focused resume should provide more context in narrative form. Instead of saying that you were on an advisory board at your local YMCA for five years, consider the following resume:

Advisory Member, YMCA, 2015 to present. *Work with a local YMCA ($5 million budget) to promote the mission of "building a healthy spirit, mind, and body for all." Our local YMCA is the epicenter and foundation for serving diverse people in our community. Our local YMCA had 20 employees and 100 volunteers when I joined the board. I started a New Initiatives Committee to expand our reach, and we now have 35 employees and over 300 volunteers. I worked with local banks and state agencies to secure funding to build a greenfield residential program with 30 people in individual and community living arrangements. We started a shelter for battered women and provided housing for people experiencing homelessness or those in transition. We created several onsite resource centers, including a counseling center and legal resources center, both staffed by pro bono professionals. We serve over 1,500 families and provide daycare and after-school programs for 175 underprivileged children. Alcoholics Anonymous* *and other community groups use our facilities. We work closely with other community non-profits, local law enforcement, and social services.*

While it's not a requirement to have a separate "board-focused" resume, we've seen many board candidates do this, especially when trying to land their first board seat. And, don't forget to include these experiences on your regular resume and your LinkedIn profile.

It can take a while to land your first board seat. First, there are far fewer new board seat opportunities than interested and available candidates. Many board seat opportunities are referral-based. To be noticed, you'll often need to reach outside your immediate network. Consider talking to those in your extended network who might be in "board influence" positions, including VCs, angel investors, or current independent directors. Engage with organizations involved in helping place board members, such as Him for Her, BoardList, Above Board, and Bolster. Highlight specific board-focused activities you're interested in engaging with, such as joining an audit committee or helping recruit other directors to the board.

Above all else, get started. Volunteer with groups you're passionate about, network with people who serve on boards, and let them know of your interest. Persistence pays off in landing a board role.

Note

1. See https://www.acellc.consulting/ (accessed January 14, 2022).

Chapter 30

Interviewing for a Board Role

By the time you get to the interview stage for a board role, you've already been partially vetted. Your references have been contacted, your resume has been confirmed, and the CEO and other board members have information on you, your accomplishments, and the skills you bring to the board. When you get called in for an interview, it's a formal step in a process that's underway, but you shouldn't expect that all you need to do is show up and answer a few softball questions. Instead, assume you're one of several finalists and that how you do in the interview will weigh heavily on whether you'll be asked to join the board. Take the interview seriously and be as prepared as possible.

The Interview

You'll probably have multiple interviews with the CEO and existing board members. You are joining a team that's just as serious and important to the company as its executive team, and the interview process will reflect that. If the company doesn't have a formalized process, consider asking to meet with several board members to do your diligence on them and better understand if you would be a fit. In this process, you benefit from learning about the company, executive team, the market, products, challenges, finances, culture, and values, just like you would when interviewing for any role.

In all good interviews, it's important to have some questions ready when you are asked, "Do you have any questions?" instead of pausing awkwardly in silence, trying to think of something clever to ask. The following are a few questions to consider:

- What is it about your experience set that the board is looking for?
- How does the board operate? Do they socialize outside board meetings, and, if so, are you expected to attend, or is it optional?
- Do they talk about issues, problems, various situations offline, or only at board meetings?
- Are they formal or informal in their meetings?
- What do they see as the company's most significant need over the next year? Two years?
- What are the strengths and weaknesses of the board?
- What are the shared values of the board?
- What is the CEO like to work with?

Understanding board governance and philosophy expectations is important and another place to probe with questions. While each board will have its own style and approach, make sure it aligns with your values.

The interview may not be the final step, as many processes include being a guest at a board meeting. In this situation, you should expect to get the same materials as everyone else and a pre-briefing with the CEO. Expect to participate just as you would if you were on the board. Be yourself. Engage with board members around issues you feel comfortable speaking about. Challenge others. Have a point of view. Simply acting in ways that you think the board or CEO wants you to behave is inauthentic at best and usually ineffective.

Diligence Items to Explore

Do your due diligence on the company while the company vets you. The following are several areas to explore:

- **Financials:** You should understand the company's financial state before you join its board. Most VC-backed startups are losing money, so it's important to understand the current cash runway and the timing for the subsequent financing. If the runway is less than six months, make sure you know the current state of the financing process and the intentions of the existing investors.

- **Glassdoor:** While Glassdoor isn't necessarily a balanced view of a company, poor company and CEO ratings, are worth understanding better through a direct conversation with the CEO.
- **Media:** Pay attention to stories and blog posts about the company, but be skeptical and use what you read as a means of asking the CEO questions rather than making judgments.
- **Board Interviews:** If the CEO doesn't have you interview other board members before deciding, ask to talk to other directors. At the minimum, you'll start building a relationship with other directors before showing up at your first board meeting.
- **Board Turnover:** It's okay to ask if the board has had other independent directors who are no longer on the board. A lot of board turnover is unusual, so if it has occurred, ask the CEO, and a former director why there's been turnover.

If you feel like something is amiss or doesn't feel right after a complete interview process, don't pursue the board seat. It's better to reject a board position before you start rather than make a multi-year commitment and, after a few meetings, realize that the board isn't a good fit for you.

Chapter 31

Your First Board Meeting

Depending on your situation, your first board meeting might be your second board meeting because you previously attended a board meeting as a trial run. You can do a few things to accelerate your impact during the onboarding process. Since a board meets infrequently, it's imperative to use the time before your first full board meeting to get up to speed so you can hit the ground running and be a fully functioning and contributing board member.

- **Understand the Company's Financials:** Probably the most important thing to know is the company's financial situation. Foundry partner and long-time CEO Chris Moody has the following thoughts for getting a board member up to speed.

Make sure the new person ramped up on the financials before attending the first meeting as an official board member by walking them through the financials line-by-line. This isn't merely about reviewing the board deck in advance, but allowing the new member to ask dumb/basic questions before the first meeting.

It'd be best to get the financials and go over them with the CFO or CEO before the first meeting. If you're unable to do that, you can still catch up quickly. Pay attention to cash burn, cash runway, the cash flow dynamics of the business, revenue and bookings growth, and key customer adoption and retention metrics. Hopefully, the company's CEO and CFO are strong enough in their board presentation development that the most important things are easy to spot and understand.

Chris Moody, Foundry, Partner

- **Have a Board Buddy:** Ask to be assigned a board buddy during or before the first meeting. Another board member will help you learn what's going on and answer questions you might have after the meeting. In addition to debriefing after the first few meetings, your board buddy can give you feedback on your engagement.

- **Learn the Corporate Structure and Governance:** Meet with the CFO and general counsel to understand the legal structure and capitalization of the company. Which decisions require board approval? Which requires shareholder approval? If the company gets acquired, how does the liquidation waterfall work? If you're a first-time board member and haven't gone to any formal training programs, make sure that you spend some time with the company lawyer to receive training or materials on governance so that you understand your fiduciary duties.

- **Meet the Team:** Try to meet with each senior team member. In addition to better putting names to faces, you'll also start to learn the structure of the leadership team. Ask for an org chart. You'll be more comfortable in the first meeting since you'll have met everyone who will be there. While genuine relationships will take time to build, a board's collective work and thinking happen in smaller groups or one-on-one interactions between formal board meetings.

- **Review the Board Packages from the Prior Year:** Ask for all the board packages and financial statements for at least the last year. Review them in detail and ask the CEO any questions about what transpired. Now that you are a board member, you're entitled to this information.

- **Get to Know the Product:** Unless you already use the company's product, have the product leaders give you a detailed demo. If you can use the product daily, buy it and use it. While most companies will provide you with access to the product for free, if it's affordable, you get bonus points for just being a regular customer, plus you learn more about the new customer experience.

- **Schedule Extra Check-ins with the CEO:** Do a before-and-after call with the CEO for the first few board meetings. Even 30 minutes for an informal chat will provide you with the additional context you might not have picked up from the meeting materials.

Ideally, every company would have a comprehensive and rigorous onboarding process for each new director. However, this is often an informal, ad-hoc process, especially at the early stages. As a new board member, you might need to drive the process to get what you need to be effective and prepared. If you document what you do, the company can use this documentation when the next director is onboarded.

Chapter 32

Communicating Effectively

Board members might have trouble making sure their voice is heard, particularly first-time board members. Your communication preferences and style impact this, but it's also inversely proportional to the number of people on the board. With three people on the board, you should have no problem making a point. With seven, you may find that speaking time is at a premium.

This challenge also varies by the nature and composition of the board. You'll feel constrained if you find yourself in a room stacked with ego-laden people demanding to be in the spotlight. You may also be aware that you're the new person to the group, the first woman, or the first person of color on the board. If you're serving on a board, the company chose you for a reason, and your views are as important as everyone else's, so you must make your voice heard.

Hopefully, your board's CEO and lead director are skilled meeting facilitators who make sure to call on every director to speak in discussions while knowing how to read a room to draw comments out of directors. But if not, here are a few suggestions for making your voice heard.

- **Communicate Issues in Advance:** No one likes to be surprised. If you have a tricky issue you want to raise at a board meeting, mention it ahead of time to the CEO. It's an effective way to be clear that you want to discuss issues.

- **Be Direct:** It's okay to interrupt, especially if the group moves from a topic you wish to address. Don't be afraid to say, "I haven't had a chance to address the situation yet."
- **Be Polite:** Go back to your elementary school days, raise your hand, and keep it raised until given a chance to speak (or use the Chat function on a Zoom call). Even the most scattered or egocentric meeting leaders cannot ignore a raised hand forever.
- **Be True to Your Style:** We've encountered every kind of board member over the years. Some express an opinion on everything. Others are introverted and hold back their comments until a discussion is well underway and they have had a chance to hear from others. Some are incredibly colorful with their use of language and metaphors. It doesn't matter what your style is—just pick one that's comfortable and natural to you.
- **Find Your Communication Niche:** One of Matt's board members at Return Path, former Oracle CFO Jeff Epstein, played a particular role in board discussions. While he would occasionally comment or express an opinion in the middle of a debate, he almost always provided the last word in a debate by saying, "Let me summarize what I've heard." He then distilled the board's discussion, recommendation, or the next action for the group. Jeff would inject some of his point of view into that summary, but the board could count on him to summarize things. Other directors find niches, such as "from the product perspective" or "first to comment." Find a niche that feels good to you.
- **Engage Between Meetings:** There are certainly times when topics come up that are followed up individually between a CEO and a board member. Individual follow-up is a helpful way to dig into something deeper without eating up valuable board meeting time and is an effective way to build rapport and trust with your CEO.
- **Ask for Feedback:** After board meetings, especially your first few, ask your CEO, your board buddy, and other directors for feedback on your participation. "Was that line of questioning helpful?," "Was that the kind of discussion you

wanted to have with the group?," "What else didn't we have a chance to cover?" Of course, once you ask for feedback, you have to be willing to learn from it.

In addition to having trouble making your voice heard, some new board members have a problem with giving difficult feedback. When you are new to a team or an organization, it's not unusual to be hesitant to be direct, especially when you are unsure of all the information and history surrounding an issue.

One approach uses inquiry over advocacy. Instead of jumping in with your feedback, as in "Well, I think. . .," start instead by asking questions and getting the other party to speak first. "What do you think about . . .?" or "Have you ever considered . . .?" is often a better way of broaching a tricky topic.

Use data to frame the conversation, such as in the Ladder of Inference framework.[1] This approach provides an objective sense of the situation. Often those involved aren't aware of the reality of the current situation, how others perceive them, or how their words or actions impact others.

A final technique helpful in raising a difficult topic is to create an option by asking, "Are you open to hearing something?" This approach is different from the direct and common approach, "We need to talk." By asking someone if they're open to hearing something, you're giving them control, and the result is usually better than starting from a confrontational position. Sometimes they'll respond with "no" or "not now," but they'll usually be ready to hear what you have to say at the moment. By reframing the difficult conversation as a choice, you'll get a greater willingness to have the conversation rather than confront immediate barriers, and resistance.

As a board member, there may be situations where you'll think, "I'm not sure this is the responsibility of the board," or, "I'm not the CEO, so I'm just going to let this play out." If you're thinking that, you're probably not the only person in the room having these thoughts. Rather than let them pass, it's worth raising the concern. Instead of ignoring conflict, or lecturing, approach difficult conversations in an open and inviting way.

Model the behavior you'd like to see in others. Don't speak over others, cut people off, or repeat what others have said with only a minor modification. Respect the people in the room, give them your full attention, and you'll get the same in return.

Note

1. Jonathan Levene, "Solving the Problem with Problem-Solving Meetings," *DCE. Harvard*, September 15, 2016. https://professional.dce.harvard.edu/blog/solving-the-problem-with-problem-solving-meetings/(accessed January 14, 2022).

Chapter 33

How to Be a Great Board Member

Since a board role is different from other roles in business, regardless of how accomplished you are, being a great board member isn't a continuation of what worked for you before. One significant difference is the infrequency of meetings, limiting your opportunities to contribute to the company. While every board differs, you can do many consistent things as a board member:

- **Be Prepared:** This means more than glancing at the materials prior to the meeting. If you only get the materials a few moments before the board meeting starts, suggest a "reading period" for everyone at the beginning of the meeting. It's a lot better to spend 15 minutes reading the materials, even if it cuts into board time, and then have a meaningful conversation rather than to go into a meeting blindly without any preparation. However, if you get materials a few days ahead of time, there's no excuse for not reading them thoroughly, taking notes, and jotting down questions you'll want to ask in the meeting. Bonus points if you share those questions with the CEO ahead of time.
- **Practice Good Meeting Hygiene:** A great board member attends all meetings, shows up on time, and doesn't leave early. Don't multitask during meetings by texting or working on your laptop or phone. Be fully engaged. If something urgent comes up, excuse yourself and leave the room. Don't return until you are fully present.

- **Have a Point of View and Speak Your Mind:** It's challenging and sometimes uncomfortable to be a contrarian or raise thorny issues, but that's one of the best things a board member can do. Your role on the board is to represent the company's interests, including many stakeholders who are absent from board meetings. Be fearless in speaking your mind. Bring up challenging and uncomfortable topics and don't work on backroom deals or tell the CEO or other board members what you think outside the meeting.
- **Be Comfortable Changing Your Mind:** Often, new information comes up during board discussions. Even if you have expressed an opinion, be open to changing your mind. It's not a sign of weakness. You have nothing to prove, and your job isn't to win the argument but rather to help the CEO get to the best decision.
- **Don't Speak to Hear Your Voice:** Not every director needs to weigh in on every discussion. If you don't have something to add to a particular conversation, either don't speak or say "I agree with what's been said," or "I agree with what Sally said." Instead, consider how your statement will add to the conversation, either by expressing a different point of view or helping move it toward a conclusion.
- **Vary Your Input:** We've seen board members who had excellent advice in their first meeting or two and then continued to repeat the same advice and the same stories in every subsequent meeting. You didn't get on a board by only carrying around a hammer, so make sure you occasionally use your wrench, screwdriver, level, and tape measure.
- **Hold the CEO Accountable:** It's common for first-time directors to fall into the trap of being afraid to hold the CEO accountable. Great board members challenge the CEO, and the best CEOs will appreciate that their board is paying attention and engaged.
- **Connect with the CEO Outside the Boardroom:** Board members are more effective when they have ongoing relationships with CEOs outside board meetings. Whether semi-regular email exchanges, periodic calls, or the occasional meal or coffee/drink, try to get to know your CEO as

a person, similar to how you'd want someone who is your manager to do with you.

- **Build Independent Relationships:** You may come into a board role not knowing anyone in the company or on the board. Work to change that dynamic immediately. The board is a team like any other team, and it works best if board members know each other and the leadership team members. You want to have a high level of trust with your fellow board members. Ideally, the CEO will encourage you to interact, socialize, and seek advice from other board members. But, instead of waiting for the CEO's permission, just take the initiative in getting to know your fellow board members.
- **Leverage Your Network, Always Be Recruiting:** Some people are naturally inclined to create open networks and look for ways to introduce people who can help each other. If this isn't a strength of yours, learn to become more so because one of the most valuable roles of a board member is connecting people and resources to the company. Connecting people can be as simple as providing your lawyer's name, some other professionals who are helpful in a situation, or being creative with the resources you have. It includes always being on the lookout for other great people to join the company. Look at every situation through the lens of, "Whom do I know who can help us?"
- **Look at Situations Strategically:** You don't need an MBA to help a company think strategically, but you do need to invest time learning about what drives the company, its strengths and weaknesses, and overall industry and competitive dynamics. To make an impact, you need to have a thorough understanding of a company's economics, competition, ecosystem, customers, and core values.
- **Be Operationally Aware:** Operational issues are highly context-dependent. You need to have a significant understanding of functional areas of the business, engage with the leader of that function, and develop a solid awareness of the day-to-day activities. Operational issues are an area where independent directors often outperform investor directors.

- **Think Outside the Box:** Good board members understand all the pieces on the chess board. Great board members play three-dimensional chess by providing advice, history, context, and then anticipating the consequences of actions. You should be able to see the proverbial forest for the trees, which can be an enormous benefit to CEOs focused on the day-to-day minutia.

Remember that it's not your job to solve the company's problems. That's the management team's job. Your job is to hold them accountable and provide ideas. Resist the temptation to get in there and fix things or tell the CEO what to do. Instead, offer context and advice, but don't dictate solutions.

Chapter 34

Conclusion

During a board meeting and the regular updating and reporting, Matt came up with one specific strategic topic about which he wanted guidance from the board. It was something that had been nagging the management team for a while without an obvious solution.

The board had a great conversation about the topic and the leadership team got specific guidance on their perspective on what to do. Matt agreed with most of it, albeit with a couple of modifications. More than anything else, he was happy for the note of clarity on an issue which he'd been struggling internally.

At the end of the discussion, Matt said, "That's a clear direction. We will go do that." At that point, one of Matt's directors, Greg Sands, politely reminded Matt that it's not the board's job to make decisions and make things happen, only to give advice and counsel. "You shouldn't take our words as gospel and assume they will work."

While the board has the final say on some items, the overwhelming majority of the company's decisions and actions are up to you and your team. You can seek guidance when you feel you need it, but it doesn't come with a guarantee that it'll work out, nor does it give you the ability to look the other way if things fail.

Boards are complex and dynamic teams. Most board members strive to help and are eager to positively impact a startup's trajectory. However, legal, psychological, and ceremonial practices, some of which are outdated or ineffective, often dictate the dynamics of a board.

Our objective in writing this book is to empower entrepreneurs with information about creating and using a board effectively. We've also tried to advise experienced, first-time, and aspiring board members.

We wrote a book we would have loved to read ourselves when we started our own companies or served on our first boards. Hopefully, this book will help you on your startup journey.

Acknowledgments

The original inspiration for the Startup Revolution series came from Brad and Mahendra's conversation in 2012. We met briefly in Ann Arbor at Brad and Jason Mendelson's event for *Venture Deals: Be Smarter than Your Lawyer and Venture Capitalist*. Mahendra followed up a few days later with an email suggesting that we write a book about boards of directors together. The *Startup Revolution* book launched a year later, with *Startup Boards* as book number four.

We published the first edition in 2013. By 2021, it was getting stale. Matt approached us about collaborating on a second edition after finishing *Startup CXO: A Field Guide to Scaling Up Your Company's Critical Functions and Teams*. Brad recently transferred management of the Startup Revolution website to Matt's new company, Bolster. Matt has extensively written about boards of directors from his experience as a long-time serial entrepreneur and someone who now helps startup CEOs build boards as part of Bolster's primary offering. We drafted Pete Birkeland, who worked on both of Matt's books and the second edition of *Do More Faster* with Brad, to give us a hand.

Many people have contributed to this book. We appreciate all the efforts, interviews, and writing from Micah Baldwin, Scott Banister, Jacques Benkoski, Paul Berberian, Rajat Bhargava, Steve Blank, Tom Bogan, Jeffrey Bussgang, Jon Callaghan, Dane Collins, Jim Dai, Aaron Easterly, Greg Gottesman, Chris Heidelberger, Will Herman, Reid Hoffman, Ben Horowitz, Richard Huston, Eric Jensen, Tracy Knox, Josh Kopelman, Clint Korver, Manu Kumar, Wendy Lea, Aileen Lee, Jim Lejeal, Seth Levine, Jocelyn Mangan, Scott Maxwell, T.A. McCann, Kelly McCracken, Ryan McIntyre, Jason Mendelson, Lesa Mitchell, Cindy Padnos, Tim Petersen, Mike Platt, Thomas Porter, Andy Rappaport, Christopher Rizik, Niel Robertson, Adam Rodnitzky, Heidi Roizen, William Ruckelshaus, Chris Rust, Lucy

Sanders, Greg Sands, Zachary Shulman, Mike Smalls, Mark Solon, Mark Suster, Shanna Tellerman, Steven Tonsfeldt, Sreeram Veeragandham, Todd Vernon, Padmasree Warrior, Noam Wasserman, Scott Weiss, and Fred Wilson.

Thanks to Bethany Crystal, Cathy Hawley, and Jenny Lawton for feedback on the second edition's structure, content, and tone. We deeply appreciate Jocelyn Mangan for writing the Foreword, introducing us to numerous female board members, and her help in changing the gender dynamics in boardrooms through Him for Her.

Special thanks to Amy Batchelor, Greg Gottesman, Seth Levine, Jason Lynch, and Ryan McIntyre for their time-consuming and extensive editing. And, once again, thanks to our editor, Bill Falloon, who shepherded this book from idea to completion.

Bibliography

Aggarwal, Dhruv, Ofer Eldar, Yael V. Hochberg, and Lubomir P. Litov, "The Rise of Dual-Class Stock IPOs." *The CLS Blue Sky Blog*, April 21, 2022. https://clsbluesky.law.columbia.edu/2021/04/21/the-rise-of-dual-class-stock-ipos/ (accessed January 7, 2022).

Ariely, Dan. *The (Honest) Truth about Dishonesty*. New York: Harper, 2012.

Blank, Steve. *The Four Steps to the Epiphany*. Pescadero, CA: K & S Ranch Press, 2013.

Blank, Steve. "Don't Give Away Your Board Seats," *WSJ*, June 13, 2013. https://www.wsj.com/articles/BL-232B-1051 (accessed January 14, 2022).

Blank, Steve and Bob Dorf. *The Startup Owner's Manual*. Pescadero, CA: K & S Ranch Press, 2012.

Blumberg, Matt. *Startup CEO: A Field Guide to Scaling Up Your Business*. 2nd edition, Hoboken, NJ: Wiley, 2020.

Blumberg, Matt. *Startup CXO: A Field Guide to Scaling Up Your Company's Critical Functions and Teams*. Hoboken, NJ: Wiley, 2021.

Bussgang, Jeff. "Board Meetings vs. Bored Meetings," *Boston VC Blog*, April 5, 2011. http://bostonvcblog.typepad.com/vc/2011/04/board-meetings-vs-bored-meetings.html (accessed January 14, 2022).

Cialdini, Robert. *Influence: Science and Practice*. Harlow: Pearson, 1984.

Coats, David. "Too Many VC Cooks in the Kitchen?," *Medium*, March 13, 2018. https://medium.com/correlation-ventures/too-many-vc-cooks-in-the-kitchen-65439f422b8 (accessed January 7, 2022).

Creary, Stephanie J., Mary-Hunter ("Mae") McDonnell, Sakshi Ghai, and Jared Scruggs, "When and Why Diversity Improves

Your Board's Performance," *Harvard Business Review*, March 27, 2019. https://hbr.org/2019/03/when-and-why-diversity-improves-your-boards-performance (accessed January 7, 2022).

de Bono, Edward. *Six Thinking Hats*. Boston: Little Brown, 1985.

Feld, Brad. "Note to CEOs: Decisions Come from You, Not the Board," *Feld Thoughts*, July 11, 2011. http://www.feld.com/wp/archives/2011/07/note-to-ceos-decisions-come-from-you-not-the-board.html (accessed January 14, 2022).

Feld, Brad. *Startup Communities: Building an Entrepreneurial Ecosystem in Your City*. Hoboken, NJ: Wiley, 2012.

Feld, Brad. "VCs Are Like D&D Characters," *Feld Thoughts*, August 2, 2012. https://feld.com/archives/2012/08/vcs-are-like-dd-characters.html (accessed January 7, 2022).

Feld, Brad, and Amy Batchelor. *Startup Life: Surviving and Thriving in a Relationship with an Entrepreneur*. Hoboken, NJ: Wiley, 2013.

Feld, Brad, and David Cohen. *Do More Faster: Techstars Lessons to Accelerate Your Startup*. 2nd edition, Hoboken, NJ: Wiley, 2019.

Feld, Brad, and Jason Mendelson. *Venture Deals: Be Smarter than Your Lawyer and Venture Capitalist*. 4th edition, 2019.

Hsieh, Tony. *Delivering Happiness: A Path to Profits, Passion, and Purpose*. New York: Grand Central Publishing, 2010.

Isaacson, Walter. *Steve Jobs*. New York: Simon & Schuster, 2011.

Kaplan, Steven N., Berk A. Sensoy, and Per Stromberg, "Should Investors Bet on the Jockey or the Horse? Evidence from the Evolution of Firms from Early Business Plans to Public Companies," *Journal of Finance*, February 2009. https://www.hhs.se/contentassets/662e98040ed14d6c93b1119e5a9796a4/kaplansensoystrombergjf2009.pdf (accessed January 15, 2022).

Kaplan, Steven, and Per Strömberg. "Financial Contracting Theory Meets the Real World: Evidence from Venture Capital Contracts," *Review of Economic Studies* 70 (2003): 281–315.

Level Playing Field Institute, "The Tilted Playing Field: Hidden Bias in Information Technology Workplaces," 2011. www.tilted_playing_field_lpfi_9_29_11.pdf (smash.org) (accessed March 3, 2022).

Levene, Jonathan "Solving the Problem with Problem-Solving Meetings," *DCE. Harvard*, September 15, 2016. https://professional.dce.harvard.edu/blog/solving-the-problem-with-problem-solving-meetings/ (accessed January 14, 2022).

Levine, Seth. "Joining the B Team," *VC Adventure,* May 18, 2016. https://www.sethlevine.com/archives/2016/05/joining-the-b-team.html (accessed January 17, 2022).

Levine, Seth. "You May Have Too Many VCs on Your Board," *VC Adventure,* March 13, 2018. https://www.sethlevine.com/archives/2018/03/you-may-have-too-many-vcs-on-your-board.html (accessed January 7, 2022).

Levine, Seth. "Designing the Ideal Board Meeting Series," *VC Adventure.* https://sethlevine.com/archives/category/designing-the-ideal-board-meeting-series (accessed January 14, 2022).

McKinsey Quarterly, "Survey on Governance." www.mckinsey.com. February 2008.

Patterson, Kerry, Joseph Grenny, Ron McMillan, and Al Switzler. *Crucial Conversations: Tools for Talking When Stakes Are High. The Business of Venture Capital.* New York: McGraw Hill, 2002.

Ramsinghani, Mahendra. *The Business of Venture Capital.* 3rd edition, Hoboken, NJ: Wiley, 2020.

Ramsinghani, Mahendra. *The Resilient Founder.* Hoboken, NJ: Wiley, 2021.

Roizen, Heidi. "We Aren't Going to Increase Diversity in the Boardroom Unless We're Willing to Appoint First-Timers. Why Is That So Hard to Do?," *Medium,* July 27, 2020. https://heidiroizen.medium.com/we-arent-going-to-increase-diversity-in-the-boardroom-unless-we-re-willing-to-appoint-first-timers-b0e456c6f8ab (accessed January 14, 2022).

Suster, Mark. "Should Your Startup Have an Advisory Board?," *Both Sides,* October 12, 2009. http://www.bothsidesofthetable.com/2009/10/12/should-your-startup-have-an-advisory-board/ (accessed January 14, 2022).

Suster, Mark. "Running More Effective Board Meetings at Startups," *Both Sides,* February 12, 2010. http://www.bothsidesofthetable.com/2010/02/12/running-more-effective-board-meetings-at-startups/ (accessed January 14, 2022).

Wasserman, Noam. *The Founder's Dilemmas.* Princeton, NJ: Princeton University Press, 2012.

Wilson, Fred "What a CEO Does," *AVC,* August 30, 2010. http://www.avc.com/a_vc/2010/08/what-a-ceo-does.html (accessed January 7, 2022).

Wilson, Fred. "The Board of Directors' Role and Responsibilities," https://avc.com/2012/03/the-board-of-directors-role-and-responsibilities/

Wilson, Fred. "Independent Director Compensation," *AVC*, August 5, 2020. https://avc.com/2020/08/independent-director-compensation/ (accessed January 7, 2022).

Index

280G. *See* US Internal
Revenue Code
409A. *See* US Internal
Revenue Code

A

Above Board, 71, 196
Acceleration provisions (compensation element), 80
Accountability, impact, 12
ACE, 195
Acquihire, concept, 172
Acquisitions. *See* Merger and acquisition
financing, 176–177
success, 173
Advisory board
board of directors, contrast, 98–99, 98t
building, 100–101
cash investment, 100
challenges, 101–102
communications, 101
expectations, management, 100
guidance, 97
member
attributes, 99–100
selection, 100
payment, 100
purpose, clarity, 100
service, 194
staffing, 101

usefulness, determination, 97
Agenda. *See* Board of directors
American Institute of Certified
Public Accountants
(AICPA)
guidelines, 166
standards, 141
Android, development, 95
Angels, 7
investors, 15
Annual calendar, creation,
113–114
Apple, success, 94–95
Appraisal rights, 41
Articles of Incorporation,
usage, 16, 40
Asset purchase, 176
Assignment for the Benefit of
Creditors (ABC), 189–190
Attorney-client privilege, 128
Audit committee
inconsistencies, 141
responsibility, 141–142
role, 35, 67

B

Banister, Scott, 101
Bankruptcies, 188–189
Basis points (BPS), financial
metric, 79
Batchelor, Amy, 8
Benefit Corp movement, 20–21
Benefit corporations, 20–21

Berberian, Paul, 35
Biases, avoidance, 72
Bid/ask gap, 177
Blank, Steve, 98, 100
Blocking rights, 19
Blue Apron, 67
Blumberg, Matt, 4, 47
    board book example, 110–111
    board existence, 12
    board meeting, course
        correction, 117
    board/observer communi-
        cations, 137
    expenses, refusal, 142
    independent directors,
        term limit, 61
    interview framework, 73–76
    jigsaw puzzle analogy, 70
    Rule of 1s, 51, 58
Board Benchmark study
    (Bolster), 78, 80, 83
Board Benchmark Survey,
    creation, 5–6
Board book, 109–113
    collaborative workspace,
        usage, 110
    dissemination, 113
    examples, 110–113
    format, consistency, 109
    PDF publication, 109
    third-party reference docu-
        ments, separation, 110
Board Buddy, usage, 88, 202
BoardList, 59, 71, 196
Board of directors, 7. *See also*
    Committees; Directors
    409A analysis, presen-
        tation, 167
    accountability, impact, 12
    advisory board, contrast,
        98–99, 98t

agenda, 127
    CEO setting, chair
        assistance, 26
audit committee, role, 35
board-focused résumé,
    usage, 196
board-ready first-timers,
    search, 83–85
building, 60
call, meeting (contrast),
    120–121
CEO performance
    assessments, 37
changes, COVID-19 pandemic
    (impact), 5
clock, chair management, 26
community organizations,
    board roles/leadership,
    194–195
company survival, 36
compensation committee,
    role, 36
composition, 47
conflict resolution, 37
control
    priorities, 37–39
    span, 41
    split, 30
corporation indemnification,
    21–22
deadlines/quality, forcing
    function (creation), 14
diversity, 81
duties
    conflicts, addressing, 18–20
    understanding, 147–148
dynamics, 57
economic priorities, 41
election, shareholder right, 40
emotional priorities, 42–43
empathy, building, 147

existence, 12
expectations, 135–136
experience, absence, 72
feedback, processing (CEO
    assistance), 27
fiduciary duty, 186–187
financial controls, estab-
    lishment, 36
founder control, dual-class
    share structures
    (usage), 40
functions, 35
governance, under-
    standing, 198
growth, stages, 57–59
illegal/fraudulent activities,
    shareholder actions
    (initiation), 41
independent board members,
    roles/responsibilities, 30
independent seats, manage-
    ment, 60–61
informal responsibilities,
    36–37
interviews, due diligence, 199
judgment, emotional priority,
    42–43
legal characteristics, 15
motions, 127
nominating/governance
    committee
    formation, 57
    role, 36
non-profit board of directors,
    role, 194
observers, 30–32
outside counsel, impact, 32
packages, review, 202
perception, 4
performance, 47
    priorities, 41

philosophy expectations,
    understanding, 198
purpose, 11
removal, 94–95
reporting guidelines
    development, 37
resignation, 94–95
responsibilities, 12–14, 42t
    understanding, 147–148
role, interview, 197–198
service, career objective, 7
situations, strategic exami-
    nation, 211
size, 47
strategic asset, 11
support, 3
transparency, emotional
    priority, 42–43
trust, emotional priority,
    42–43
turnover, due diligence, 199
types, 11–12
venture capitalists
    interviews, 76
    presence, value, 49
    relationships, 53
votes, 127
Board of directors, meetings
    agenda, 107–108
    call, contrast, 120–121
    counsel, interaction, 15
    critical items, focus, 108–109
    decisions, positive/negative
        aspects (balance), 138
    dinner, supply, 116
    director seating, 115–116
    disagreements, 129–130
    discussion/decision
        item, 118–119
    dynamics, 115
    finalist audition, 75

Board of directors, meetings
  (*Continued*)
 food, availability, 115
 formal items, consid-
  eration, 130
 hybrid meetings,
  usage, 121–123
 hygiene, practice, 209
 initiation, 201
 interactions, 193–194
 lawyer/outside counsel,
  attendance, 128
 length, 116
 management teams,
  interaction, 6
 minutes, taking, 127, 131
 news, communication,
  136–138
 post meeting, 124–125
  engagement, 206–207
  survey, 123–124
 preparation, 105
  value, 106
 remote attendees, involvement, 121–123
 seating, rule, 115–116
 slides, usage (consider-
  ation), 118
 story, crafting, 106
 strategies, brainstorming, 109
 surprises, problem, 137
 team, inclusion, 117–118
 unanimous written consent,
  131–132
 video conferencing, challenges, 121–123
 voting, mechanics, 128–129
Board of directors, members, 7
 advisory board member
  complement, 99

 attributes, 69
 candidate proposal, 82
 communication, 205
 company roles, 58t
 fiduciary duties, 38
  defining, duty of care/
   loyalty (impact), 17
 honesty, 64
 independent relationships,
  building, 211
 input, variation, 210
 learning by doing, 147–148
 legal duties, 16–18
 meeting hygiene, practice, 209
 mentor role, advice, 146
 network, leverage, 211
 operational awareness, 211
 personal liability, risk
  (absence), 188
 point of view, 210
 preparation, 193, 209
 quality/performance, 209
 recruitment/interview, 71
 rejection, 75–76
 removal, 91
 roles, 25
 skills, 68t
 sourcing, 71–73
 speaking, 210
 trusted relationship, 146
 types, 91
Boardroom
 CEO connection, 210–211
 dynamics, 19
Bolster, 5–6, 59, 61, 71–73, 147
 board 360 evaluation
  process, 92
 Board Benchmark study,
  78, 80, 83
 Board Book, 110–111

board position, assistance, 193
company email, usage, 137
engagement, 196
impact, 84
Miller, impact, 84–85
Bolster Networks, 72
Brainstorming, usage, 109
Bridge loan, 162
Buffett, Warren, 69
Business
closure/cessation, 185
growth, board concerns, 136
judgment rule, application, 18
opportunities, 73
Business of Venture Capital, The
(Mahendra), 91
Bussgang, Jeff, 120
Bylaws, usage, 16

C

Callaghan, Jon, 17, 18
Campbell, Bill, 95
Capital
first round, raising, 53–54
investment, 55
Cap table (cleanliness), outside
counsel role, 34
Carve-outs, 173
Cash flow solvency, balance sheet
solvency (contrast), 185
Cash resources, impacts, 22
C Corps, governance
philosophy, 21
Chair (lead director)
becoming, decision, 29
board member roles, 25–27
characteristics, 26–27
facilitator/communicator
role, 26
role, 27. *See also* Executive chair.

term, usage, 7
Change of control, 80
Chapter 7 bankruptcy,
avoidance, 189
Chapter 11 bankruptcy, 188–189
Chief Executive Officer (CEO)
accountability, 210
alternate, availability, 153
board feedback processing, 27
board firing, reasons, 152–153
board of directors
expectations, 135–136
performance assessment, 37
changes, situations, 149–150
check-ins, scheduling, 2032
connection, 210–211
control freak, problem, 152
directionally challenged, 152
economic/performance
priorities, 41
executive team disagreements,
13–14
expenses, 142–143
financing challenges, board
questions, 150
news, communication,
136–138
performance, metrics
(establishment), 154
responsibilities, 42t
scaling, 151
absence, 152–153
term, usage, 7
transitions, 149
planning, 154
Cisco WebEx, 120
Claims, filing (process), 23
C-level experience, absence, 72
Closed Session, usage, 108,
111, 119–120

Co-founder
  role, 48
  struggle, 75
Committees
  compensation, 140–141
  IPO involvement, 180
  meeting formalities, 139–140
  role, 35–36
  usage, 139
Common stock, fair market
      value (FMV) determina-
      tion, 165–166
Communication
  directness/politeness, 206
  effectiveness, 205
  niche, finding, 206
  style, 206
Community organizations,
      board roles/leadership,
      194–195
Company
  acquihire, 172
  acquisition
    board approval, 177, 177t
    financing, 176–177
  board alignment, chair
      (impact), 26
  board members, role, 58t
  capitalization, familiarity, 87
  cash levels, decrease, 186
  due diligence, 198–199
  financials, understanding, 201
  financings participation, 58
  founders, absence, 151
  legal structure, familiarity, 87
  post-deal integration, 178
  public company boards,
      venture capitalists
      (presence),
      181–182
  purchase, 175

  deal, negotiation/
      structuring, 175–176
  representation, outside
      counsel role, 33
  sale, 169
    negotiation, bid/ask gap, 177
    outside counsel, role,
      171–172
    shareholder representative,
      role, 173–174
  solvency, 185
  stock option grant, 78
  survival, board of directors
      responsibility, 36
  trajectory, change, 73
  transaction, management, 178
Company Six, 35
Compensation, 77
  package, elements, 80
  private company directors,
      stock compensation, 79
  stock-based compensation, 79
Compensation committee,
      role, 36
Confidential filing, 180
Confidentiality, 169–170
  agreement, usage, 169
  IPO confidentiality, 180
  quiet period, 180
Conflict resolution, board
      of directors respon-
      sibility, 37
Control
  change of control, 80
  loss, 64
  priorities, 37–39
Convertible notes, usage, 162
Cooley, 15, 32, 34
Corporate books/records,
      inspection (shareholder
      rights), 40

Corporate directors, McKinsey
study, 108
Corporate structure/governance,
learning, 202
Corporations
benefit corporations, 20–21
general liability coverage
insurance policy, 23
Correlation Ventures
study, 49, 50f
Co-sale rights, 141
Costanoa Ventures,
109, 136, 213
Counsel. *See* Outside counsel
selection, 23
COVID-19 pandemic, impact, 5
Creative thinking, 99
Creditors, board responsibility,
186–187
Crucial Conversations (Patterson/
Grenny/McMillan/
Switzler), 108
Crystal, Bethany, 72
Customer-type experience
(directors), 67

D
Deadlines/quality, forcing
function (creation), 14
Debt. *See* Venture debt
Defense costs, consideration, 22
DeGolia, Karen, 27
Delaware, legal framework, 20
deSPAC transaction/process,
182–183
Diligent, board 360 evaluation
process, 92
Directors. *See* Independent
director; Investor
board/board-equivalent
experience, 66

board of director fit, 64–65
candidates, due diligence, 74
characteristics, search, 63
check-in, 89
company need, 65
constructive conversation, 93
customer-type experience, 67
detached/objective view,
usage, 147
domain expertise, 67
entrepreneurial experience,
66–67
experiences, 66–68
fiduciary duty, imposition, 186
functional experience, 67–68
in-person interaction, encour-
agement, 88
onboarding, 87, 88–89
package, preparation, 88
option grant size, 79t
profile, assembly, 72
responsibility, 69–70
skills, 63–64
stage transition experience, 67
strengths/weaknesses, consideration, 65
team, interaction, 89
topics, exploration, 108
types, 47–48
Directors and officers (D&O)
coverage, nonduplication, 23
indemnification, 41
cost, 22
insurance
compensation element, 80
usage, question, 21–23
wrongdoings, 22
Dissenters, rights, 41
Diversity, differences, 82–83
Domain expertise
(directors), 67

Down round, 41
  occurrence, 161
Downside cases, 172
Dual-class shares structures,
  usage, 39–40
Duty of care, 17, 97
Duty of care/loyalty
  impact, 17
  legal concepts, 15
Duty of confidentiality, 17
Duty of disclosure, 17, 18
Duty of loyalty, 17, 97

E
Early investors/VCs, impact, 19
Early-stage boards, 194–195
  conflicts, 130
Early-stage companies, founders
  (presence), 92
Earn-outs, 177
Easterly, Aaron, 112–113
Ellison, Larry, 95
Emotional balance (board
  member attribute), 69
Emotional quotient (EQ), 27
Emotional stability (advisory
  board member), 99
Empathy, building, 147
Employees
  board treatment,
    importance, 187
  onboarding, guide/usage, 87
Energize Colorado, 81
Enron (scandal), 29
Entrepreneur
  accomplishments, 39
  adult supervision, 53
  private session, value, 120
  term, usage, 7
Epstein, Jeff, 206
Equilar, board 360 evaluation
  process, 92

Equity instrument (compensation element), 80
Executive chair, role, 28–29
Executive Session, 119–120
  confidential memos, 110, 111
  usage, 108
Executive teams, executive
  recruitment/hiring/
  firing, 65

F
Fable, 108
Facebook
  Class A/Class B ownership,
    percentages, 39
  share class creation, 39
Fair market value (FMV), 165
  discrepancy, 167
Fear, culture (creation), 91
Feedback, 93, 207
  CEO need, 106
  delivery, 69
  follow-up, 124
  real-time feedback, 105
  receiving, 121
FeedBurner, 5
Feld, Brad
  blog, 53
  board of director meeting,
    seating arrangement, 116
Fiduciary duty, 16–17, 19–20, 38
Fiduciary responsibility, 170
Financial controls, establishment (board of directors
  responsibility), 36
Financial returns, investor
  importance, 54
Financials
  company financials, under-
    standing, 201
  due diligence, 198–199
  review, 88

Financing, 159
  acquisition financing, 176–177
  bridge loan, usage, 162
  convertible notes, usage, 162
  documents, alignment, 59
  down round, 161
  insider-led round, 160–161
  new investor-led
      round, 159–160
  raising process, 54
  rights offering, 161
  ventural capitalist (VC)
      involvement, degree, 161
  venture debt, usage, 162–163
Findley, Linda, 67
Firm, stability, 55
Flatiron Partners, 55
Flybridge Capital Partners, 120
Forcing function, creation, 14
Formal items, consideration, 130
Founder
  absence, 151
  content/advice/
      introductions, 13
  controls, 38, 40
  director, removal, 92
  friendliness, 40
  role, 25, 47–49
  seat, presence, 31
  term, usage, 7
  VC due diligence, 54
Founder/CEO
  outside counsel, interaction
      (absence), 19
  title, 7
Founder's Dilemmas, The
      (Wasserman), 38
Foundry, 21, 49, 53–54,
      56, 87, 201
Four Steps to the Epiphany, The
      (Blank), 100

Fraudulent transfers, board
      member approval, 188
Freeman, Brenda, 50, 51
Front-loaded grant, 79
Functional experience
      (directors), 67–68

G
Glaros, Nicole, 146
Glassdoor, 199
Going public, 179
Goodwin Law, 171, 172
Google, 95
  dual-class approach, 39
Google Doc, 110
Google Drive, 110
Google Forms, usage, 123
Google Meet, 120
Gore, Al, 95
Governance, learning, 202
Governance philosophy, 21, 69–70
Greylock, 28, 29
Groupon, dual-class share
      structures, 39
Growth
  deceleration, CEO
      (impact), 149–150
Growth, stages, 57–59
GrubHub, 115

H
Hart-Scott-Rodino (HSR)
      regulatory filings, 183
Hastings, Reed, 69
Havenly, 107
Hawley, Cathy, 72
Hester, Jaclyn, 56
Him for Her, 59, 71, 195, 196
Hoffman, Reid, 29
Hsieh, Tony, 150
Huston, Richard, 36
Hybrid meetings, 121–123

I

Illuminate Ventures, 82
Indemnification, components,
    21–22
Independence rules, 180
Independent board members,
    roles/responsibilities, 30
Independent director, 48, 50
  compensation, 78–80
  early appointment, 83
  removal, 93–94
  talent pool, characteristic, 84
  term limits, 61
Independent seats, manage-
    ment, 60–61
Informal advisory role,
    presence, 194
Initial public offering
    (IPO), 179
  approach, 142
  committees, involvement, 180
  confidentiality, 180
  consideration, 67–68
  growth company prep-
    aration, 57
  insider status, 181
  process, 179
  VC-backed founders,
    presence, 151
  venture capitalist (VC)
    presence/exit,
    reasons, 181–182
In-person interaction, encour-
    agement, 88
In-room setup, problems, 122
Insider-led rounds, 160–161
Insiders, board member
    status, 181
Institutional investors, 48
Integrity (board member
    attribute), 69

Intellectual property (IP),
    purchase, 176
Intentional bias, absence, 82
Intentional harm, sub-
    jectivity, 22
Internal Revenue Code. *See* US
    Internal Revenue Code
Interviews
  board interview,
    197–198
  data collection, 74
  due diligence, 199
  finalists, audition, 75
  multiple/video meetings,
    usage, 73–74
  process, 73–76
  questions, 198
  references, checking, 74
    questions, 74
  rejections, 75–76
  selling process, 75
  seriousness, 73
Intuit, 95
Investment risk, 187
Investor
  board members, limitation,
    59–60
  conversion rights, 38
  director, 48, 49
    compensation, avoidance,
    77–78
    removal, 92–93
  financial returns, 54
  protective provisions, 38
  skills/mindset, advisory
    board member com-
    plement, 99
  term, usage, 8
IronPort Systems, 101
Isaacson, Walter, 95
Issues, communication, 205

J

Jensen, Eric, 15, 105
Job description, creation, 71
JOBS Act of 2012, 180
Jobs, Steve, 94–95
Joyeux Advisors, 50, 51

K

Kaden, Rebecca, 16
Kaplan, Steven, 151
Kirby, Eric, 175
Korver, Clint, 11
Kumar, Manu, 153

L

Ladder of Inference
    framework, 207
Lame-duck board, 11–12
Late investors/VCs,
    impact, 19–20
Lauchengo, Martina, 109
Lawson, Jeff, 11
Lawyer, term (usage), 8
Lead director. *See* Chair
Lea, Wendy, 81
Legacy company, board member
    (impact), 51
Levine, Seth, 49
Levitt, Arthur, 95
Limited Liability Companies
    (LLCs), governance
    philosophy, 21
Limited partners (LPs), 77
    fiduciary duty, 170
    management fees, 78
LinkedIn
    CEO roles/responsibilities,
        28–29
    dual-class share structures, 39
Long-term commitment (advi-
    sory board member), 99
Long-term vision, 75

M

Management
    director, 47, 48–49
    operational work, 64–65
    outside counsel
        engagement, 33
    team member, inclusion, 48
    teams, board of directors
        (interaction), 6
Mangan, Jocelyn, 30
Material nonpublic information,
    disclosure, 170
Mayer, Lee, 107
Media, usage/due dil-
    igence, 199
Mendelson, Jason, 4, 54
Mentors/mentorship, 145–147
    peer-mentorship, 146
Merger, 176
Merger and acquisition
    (M&A)
    lawyers, involvement,
        171–172
    transaction, confidentiality
        agreement (usage), 169
Metrics, summary, 105
Microsoft, 28–29, 108
Microsoft Teams, 120
Miller, Cristina, 84–85
Miller, Tim, 109, 136, 151
Mindset (board member
    attribute), 69
Minutes, taking, 127, 131
Mitchell, Lesa, 73
Moody, Chris, 87, 201
Morgan Stanley, Shareworks/
    Option Impact, 140
Motions, 127
    motion to table/motion to
        postpone, 129
Moz, 5

N

NASDAQ, board 360 evaluation
    process, 92
Network, leverage, 211
New investor-led
    rounds, 159–160
News, communication, 136–138
News Corp, dual-class share
    structures, 39
Nominating/governance
    committee, 142
  formation, 57
  role, 36
Non-disclosure agreement
    (NDA), usage, 169
Non-investor shareholders,
    control, 38
Non-profit board of directors,
    role, 194
No-shop agreement, usage, 169

O

Observers, 30–32
  rights, delineation, 31
  seats, limitation/
    elimination, 49
Ohio TechAngels, 36
Onboarding, 87
  package, preparation, 88
Ongoing communication,
    management, 135
Open-ended questions,
    avoidance, 109
Operational Update, 114
Option grant
  calculation, 79
  stock option grants, 78, 165
Oracle, 95, 205
Organizations, Robert's Rules of
    Order (usage), 128
Outside counsel, 32

board of directors
  engagement, 33
  interaction, 15
cap table cleanliness, 34
company sale role,
    171–172
company/stockholder repre-
    sentation, 33
constructive feedback,
    request, 34
criticism, openness, 34
management, engagement, 33
meeting attendance, 128
objectives, 33–34
term, usage, 8

P

Padnos, Cindy, 82
Parachute payment, 173
Partner, tenure, 55
Passive-aggressive member,
    impact, 91
Path Forward, 5
Patterns, matching, 13
Peer-mentorship, 146
Peer network, building, 148
Performance, earn-outs, 177
Personal liability, risk
    (absence), 188
Personnel, exodus
    (indications), 150
Pit bull, impact, 91
Platt, Mike, 32–34
Porfido, Meg, 124
Portfolio, strength, 55–56
Positive attitude (advisory
    board), 99
Post meeting, 124–125
survey, 123–124
Post-Termination Exercise
    Period (PTEP), 94

Private company directors, stock compensation, 79
Private equity (PE) firms, compensations, 77–78
Private Investment in Public Equity (PIPE), 182–183
Private session, value, 120
Product, knowledge, 202
Product-led growth (PLG), 67
Protective provisions, 38
Public Benefit Corporations (PBCs), 16, 20–21
Public Company Accounting Oversight Board (PCOAB) standards, 141
Public company boards, venture capitalists (presence), 181–182

Q
Quiet period, 180
Quorum, 127

R
Racial diversity, 82–83
Reading period, usage, 209
Reboot, board 360 evaluation process, 92
Rees, Joanna, 66
Remote attendees, meeting involvement, 121–123
Remote participant, disengagement, 121–122
Reorganizational bankruptcies, 189
Repayment, primary source, 162
Reporting board, 11–12
Reporting guidelines, board of directors development, 37
Responsiveness (advisory board), 99

Résumés, gaps, 72
Return Path, 5, 118, 147
board discussions, 206
board member
exit, 55
joining, 73, 106
directors, presence, 47
expenses, nonapproval, 142
insider-led rounds, 160
memos, usage, 110
merger, 175
Revenue (growth stage), 57–59
Rights offering, 161
Rights of first refusal (ROFRs), 141
Robert, Henry Martyn, 127
Robert's Rules of Order, 127–128
Roizen, Heidi, 85
Rover, board book example, 111–113
Rule of 1s (Blumberg), 51, 58

S
SAFE, 162
Sands, Greg, 136, 213
Sarbanes-Oxley legislation, impact, 29
Schmidt, Eric, 95
Securities and Exchange Commission (SEC), 95, 179
public company bonus rules, 16
Senior executive, firing, 94
Sequoia, 150
Series A/Series B revenue, raising, 47
Shareholder Rights Agreement, 40

Shareholders
board responsibility, 187–188
impact, 21
non-investor shareholders,
control, 38
pricing, fairness, 160
representative, company sale
role, 173–174
rights, 40–41
value, maximization, 69–70
Shares, dual-class approach, 39
Shareworks/Option Impact
(Morgan Stanley), 140
Simons, Alessandra, 171, 172
Special Purpose Acquisition
Company (SPAC), 182–183
acquisition, 141
deSPAC transaction/process,
182–183
Sphero, 35
Spotify, 108
Stage transition, director
expertise, 67
Stakeholder structures,
differences, 29
Stanford University, 11
Startup (growth stage), 57–59
Startup boards
issues/challenges, 6
structure/composition/
approach, 3
Startup CEO (Blumberg),
4, 12, 151
Startup Communities (Feld), 5
Startup CXO (Blumberg), 5
Startup Life (Feld/Batchelor), 8
Startups
cash constraints, 22
control levels, 38
coverage, minimum, 22
journey, 54

Status quo, acceptance
(problem), 81–82
Stock-based compensation, 79
Stockholders, outside counsel
role, 33
Stock option grants, 78, 165
Suster, Mark, 100, 114

T
Team
board of directors meeting
inclusion, 117–118
meeting, 202
Team, director interaction, 89
Techstars, 5, 73, 84, 146, 194
Term sheet, approach, 54
Thinking, organization, 13
Third-party service provider,
assets/liabilities
(assigning), 190
Threshold Ventures, 85
Training, courses/seminars
(availability), 195
Transactional activity,
support, 14
True Ventures, 17
Twilio, 11
Twitter, 16, 121

U
UberEats, 115
Ulu Ventures, 11
Unanimous written consent,
131–132
Unconscious bias, 81–83
Union Square Ventures,
16, 54, 79
Upfront Ventures, 100
US Internal Revenue Code
Section 280G, 173
Section 409A, 165, 167
analysis, presentation, 167

V

Valuation firm, evaluation (questions), 166–167
Venture Capital Executive Compensation Survey (VCECS), 140
Venture capitalist (VC), 48
  blocking rights, 19
  board members
    focus, 17
    means returns, 50f
    service, 135
  board of directors, relationship, 53
  compensation, 77
  conflict, transparency, 18–19
  due diligence, 54
  exists, demonstration, 55–56
  fiduciary duty, 170
  financial/stability/stature, 56
  financing involvement, degree, 161
  interviews, 76
  investment risk, 187
  investor groups, partnerships, 14
  number, limit, 49
  operator recruitment, 59–60
  partner, support, 31
  term, usage, 8
Venture Deals (Feld/Mendelson), 4–5, 37, 56, 59, 159, 174
Venture debt
  lending, banks (role), 188
  usage, 162–163
Veripost, merger, 175
Vesting period (compensation element), 80
Viacom, dual-class share structures, 39

Video conferencing
  challenges, 121–123
  impact, 121
  in-room setup, problem, 122
  remote participant, disengagement, 121–122
  votes, recording difficulty, 129
Vontier, 27
Votes, 127
Voting
  mechanics, 128–129
  rights, 40
Voting Agreement, usage, 92
Vulnerability, 145–147

W

Warrior, Padmasree, 108
Wasserman, Noam, 38, 39, 151
Weiner, Jeff, 28–29
West Ventures, 66
Wilson, Fred, 54–55, 79, 123, 150, 175
Wind-down, 188
Working board, 11–12
Written communication skills, improvement, 75
Wrongful acts, policy definition, 22

Y

Yelp, dual-class share structures, 39

Z

Zappos, exit (success), 150
Zone of insolvency, 163, 185–186
Zoom, 120
  Chat function, usage, 206
Zuckerberg, Mark, 39
Zynga, dual-class share structures, 39